MAX NEWNHAM

Tax for
Small Business

MAX NEWNHAM

Tax for Small Business

A Survival Guide

W
Wrightbooks

First published 2008 by Wrightbooks

an imprint of John Wiley & Sons Australia, Ltd

42 McDougall Street, Milton Qld 4064

Office also in Melbourne

Typeset in Granjon 12/15 pt

© Max Newnham 2008

The moral rights of the author have been asserted.

National Library of Australia Cataloguing-in-Publication data:

Author:	Newnham, Max.
Title:	Tax for small business : a survival guide / Max Newnham.
ISBN:	9780731408344 (pbk.)
Notes:	Includes index.
Subjects:	Small business — Taxation — Australia.
Dewey number:	336.2070994

Printed by McPherson's Printing Group

10 9 8 7 6 5 4 3 2 1

Disclaimer

The material in this publication is of the nature of general comment only, and neither purports nor intends to be advice. Readers should not act on the basis of any matter in this publication without considering (and if appropriate taking) professional advice with due regard to their own particular circumstances. The author and publisher expressly disclaim all and any liability to any person, whether a purchaser of this publication or not, in respect of anything and of the consequences of anything done or omitted to be done by any such person in reliance, whether in whole or in part, upon the whole or any part of the contents of this publication.

Contents

Acknowledgements

To write a book like this that deals with a highly technical subject such as tax requires a lot of research and help. Several people helped to ensure that I did not wander too far from the letter of the law in search of the vibe:

- Max Warlow from Max Warlow and Associates Pty Ltd was invaluable when it came to help with GST and the taxes levied by the states and territories.

- John Sesto and Sasho Slaveski from J P Sesto and Associates, being lawyers, kept me on the right side of the law when it came to income tax generally, and more particularly the small business capital gains tax concessions.

- Andrew Pugsley from TaxBiz Australia Pty Ltd read over the chapter on FBT and made sure that it was not only technically correct but also had all of the commas in the right places.

- Kristen Hammond from John Wiley & Sons Australia Ltd made sure that some of the more technical chapters made sense and did not become a good cure for insomnia.

- Lastly my wife Liz once again shouldered more than her fair share of the domestic duties while I wrote the book.

CHAPTER 1

Tax through the ages

Business owners who ignore their tax obligations can end up suffering in different ways. They can end up paying too much tax due to not organising their affairs properly, or even worse, be audited by the Australian Taxation Office (ATO) and discover too late that they have made mistakes that result in large fines and penalties.

In trying to understand how tax affects a business, it helps to have an understanding of how tax has been imposed over the years, and how people in the past have tried to find ways of minimising the impact of one of the inevitabilities of life. When you look at the history of taxation, you realise, in fact, that with its first imposition came tax minimisation and avoidance. Tax avoidance is effectively cheating a government of its tax revenue by, for example, not declaring cash sales. Tax minimisation, on the other hand, is a person or business organising their affairs, within the law, to pay the lowest amount of tax possible. This principle was first backed by an eminent British judge in the 1800s, who ruled that 'it was everyone's right to organise their affairs so that they did not pay the maximum amount of tax'.

Taxation BC

Income tax as we know it today is a relatively new innovation, but tax has been around in other forms for thousands of years.

One of the earliest examples was a tax on the consumption of cooking oil in the time of the Egyptian pharaohs. The scribes charged with collecting the tax visited households to ensure the occupants were not using lard or other forms of fat instead of oil—and thus paying less tax.

The Romans also levied taxes, including customs duties at ports, on both imports and exports, and an inheritance tax that was used to provide funds for retired soldiers. Julius Caesar imposed a 1 per cent tax on the sale of slaves that was eventually increased to 4 per cent.

Taxation in Great Britain and beyond

The earliest forms of tax in Great Britain were imposed on products and land. The land taxes took many forms: one was based on the land area a house occupied, another on the number of windows a house had. This last tax led to an early form of tax minimisation by homeowners—they bricked up windows. It may have meant less light for the house, but at least they were minimising tax!

Even a feature of the distinctive Tudor-style houses was prompted by a desire to minimise tax. These houses are famed for their use of painted white panels with wood, but many also have a ground floor smaller than the upper storeys, which creates a wide overhang over the street. Evidently, this was done because the less land the ground floor occupied, the lower the property taxes were.

The earliest form of income tax was first introduced in Great Britain to finance the war against Napoleon in 1799. There was an annual tax-free threshold of £60, with a tax rate of 10 per cent on incomes above that. Not surprisingly, it was an unpopular tax that many people found ways to avoid, and instead of collecting the expected £10 million in the first year, the British government only got £6 million.

When a peace treaty was signed with France the tax was repealed, but then reintroduced when war broke out again. It is this second tax act that is the model for most modern tax systems. In addition to imposing tax on different classes of income, such as property, farming, retirement annuities, self-employed and wages, there was also a withholding tax on interest income paid by the Bank of England.

This second version of income tax was, again, extremely unpopular, and after the victory at Waterloo it was not only repealed, but all records associated with it destroyed. Although unpopular, its design had been shown to be one of the fairest ways to impose income tax, in that those less fortunate paid less tax.

The income tax system currently operating in the UK was introduced in 1842 as another temporary tax, supposedly for only three years. Even today it's still a temporary tax that expires each year on 5 April, and must be reapplied by an annual finance act.

The history of American income tax is similar to that of the UK. Income-tax legislation based on the original English 1799 tax was drawn up to fund the war of 1812, but never imposed. It wasn't until the Civil War that a progressive income tax was actually introduced. Again, tax avoidance must have been high, as only 276 661 people filed tax returns in 1870, out of a total population of approximately 38 million!

Australia's taxation experience

Australia's experience with taxation has been very similar to that of other countries. The original taxes were on goods and services and not income, and, as in the UK and USA, income tax was introduced to fund involvement in a war.

Tax in the colonies

Tax revenue in Australia has mainly been used to fund government facilities and services. The first taxes were introduced by the Colony of New South Wales to help pay for the completion of Sydney's first gaol, and to provide funds for the care of the colony's orphans. As the government provided more benefits, taxes were increased to fund them.

Just as there has been controversy in recent years about the imposition of new taxes and the sale of government assets, there was also opposition to taxes in the early days of the colonies.

Often the major reason for opposition to new taxes was their regressive and inequitable nature: the people who had the least tended to pay a much higher proportion than the more wealthy. To avoid this criticism, taxes were initially imposed on goods such as tobacco and alcohol on supposedly moral grounds.

It was when the colonies started taxing non-luxury items like tea, sugar, flour and rice that low-income earners started paying an inequitable share of the total tax take. This prompted some discontent; but it was nothing compared to the trouble caused by a tax imposed during the gold rush. With the amount of wealth being produced from gold, it had been decided to charge all miners a license fee. The fee was incredibly unpopular. It was imposed at a high rate, the miners could not see how they benefited from the revenue raised, it was not linked to gold discoveries and, by comparison, wealthy landowners paid very little tax.

Discontent was expressed by everything from avoidance measures such as hiding from the fee-collectors, to open revolt at the Eureka Stockade. That protest, although extreme, did achieve its aim, with the miner's fee being scrapped and replaced by an export tax on gold.

Eventually, the colonies imposed their own forms of income tax. Tasmania was the first: in 1880 it introduced a tax on the profits of public companies. This was followed four years later by South Australia imposing a general income tax, and by New South Wales in 1895.

As Australia's population grew, each of the colonies introduced more taxes. These taxes often differed between the colonies, either by their rate or what they were charged on. With Federation some of this confusion and variation was removed.

Taxation after Federation

The first taxes handed over to the Commonwealth were customs and excise duties. Even though a federal income tax was imposed in 1915, it was not until 1942 that the Commonwealth started collecting all income taxes. Two years later, to help maintain a more regular flow of tax revenue, group tax and provisional tax were introduced. These taxes still exist today, but are called Pay As You Go (PAYG) withholding and instalments tax.

Over the years since Federation, many taxes have been introduced and then withdrawn or changed. In 1917, an entertainment tax was introduced on the admission price of all entertainment, and led to tax auditors setting up camp at race meetings, theatres and cinemas to ensure there was no tax avoidance.

Sales tax was introduced on specified items in 1930, and was an indirect tax paid by wholesalers, as opposed to being paid by the end consumer. Then in 1942, a uniform income tax was introduced across the whole of Australia, collected by the Commonwealth Government and then distributed to the States and Territories. In 1944, the Commonwealth Government brought in the Pay As You Earn (PAYE) system for collecting tax from employees, and the provisional tax system for people who earned investment and business income.

Changes in the 1980s

For almost 40 years, Australia's tax system did not undergo any major changes. Then, in 1983, the tax system entered a short period of almost constant change. The first was the introduction of the prescribed payments system in 1983. This imposed a tax collection system similar to PAYE on people working as contractors in the building industry.

On 20 September 1985, capital gains tax (CGT) was introduced to stop perceived tax avoidance on the profits made when assets and investments were sold. The unusual start date was when the Commonwealth Budget was handed down. This system of handing down the Budget after the start of each financial year led to many tax changes being introduced part-way through the year — including changes to tax rates, which created an administrative nightmare. Thankfully, someone recognised how crazy this system was, and the Commonwealth Budget began to be handed down in May instead.

With the introduction of fringe benefits tax (FBT) and the Medicare levy, 1986 proved to be a busy year. The Medicare levy was introduced to provide funds for Australia's health system; the FBT system was introduced to tax employees on benefits taken in a form other than salaries or wages.

Over time, the ATO has used the broad powers given to it under the FBT system to attack almost any benefit it wanted to, including frequent flyer benefits. Some have said the ATO uses the FBT system to attack any benefits that employees of the commercial world get and public servants don't.

Introducing the GST

For 14 years after the introduction of FBT and the Medicare levy, there was not much in the way of change, apart from alterations to tax rates and the taxing of superannuation (a completely different subject, explained in my book *Super Made Simple: A Survival Guide*).

Then 1 July 2000 saw the most radical overhaul of Australia's taxation system ever undertaken. Not only were the GST and PAYG systems introduced and sales tax, PAYE and provisional tax withdrawn, legislation was also introduced to limit who could claim business losses, which defined who was regarded as running a business.

What changes to the taxation system will be made over the coming years is anybody's guess, especially given the 2007 change of government. All I know for sure is, it won't be a matter of *if* tax changes will be made, but *when*.

Trusting in history

One of the most popular business structures used today is a discretionary family trust. Due to their tax benefits, they are often attacked as the root of all evil when it comes to tax avoidance, and you could be forgiven for thinking they're a recent invention designed to foil the Australian Taxation Office. In fact, as well as providing tax benefits, they've been used for hundreds of years and are a legitimate business and investment structure available to anyone.

Trusts trace their ancestry back to the Middle Ages: they were first embraced by the English in the 12th century to avoid the tax excesses of the king. Instead of lodging a yearly tax return or a quarterly business activity statement (BAS), the farmers of that time had to endure weekly visits from tax collectors.

There was no self-assessment. The peasant farmers would be assessed on the spot: the tax collector decided how much tax was owed, and took with him whatever livestock and money would pay the debt. In those days there was no right of objection, and definitely no administrative appeals board. Taxpayers were faced with weekly, not yearly, increases.

In an effort to protect the rewards of their hard work, some farmers approached the Church with a proposal. They'd give the Church title to their land and property under several conditions: they would retain the right to use the land, to buy and sell the land and property, and to pass the land to their first-born sons. The Church accepted the offer, and thousands of farmers entrusted it with their land—hence the name 'trust'. The next time the tax collector visited, he was greeted with the news that the farm was now owned by the Church, and since the Church was exempt from paying tax, he left empty-handed.

However, in what can only be described as a salutary lesson for anyone engaged in tax-avoidance schemes, many of these medieval tax dodgers lost out and the Church benefited.

When the bubonic plague hit Europe, the Church became very wealthy from the land it inherited under these trusts.

In feudal England, trusts were also used by men who did not have a son. Under the law of the time, if a man died without a son over the age of 21, the right to use and earn income from the property passed to his local lord. In addition, if he had daughters the lord could marry them off to anyone he wanted. For lords with unattractive or idiot sons, this must have proved a valuable non-taxable fringe benefit.

To avoid this, a man would ask some trustworthy friends to hold the land for him until he either had a son who reached the age of 21 or one of his daughters married. It was more an estate-planning scheme than a tax-planning one.

In 1535, the king and his nobles challenged the legality of trusts and attempted to ban them, but the judges of the Chancery Court (the equivalent of our High Court) upheld the validity of the trust concept. In 1536 the Statute of Uses was passed, cementing trusts in English law. Many legal scholars regard this legislation as the greatest achievement of Anglo-Saxon jurisprudence.

Since the Middle Ages, trusts have been used for the twin purposes of reducing income tax and death taxes. Here in Australia, when death duties existed, trusts were a popular way of overcoming probate problems. People transferred assets that increased in value, such as property and shares, into a trust, so that a limit was placed on the value of an individual's estate and death duties were reduced.

To understand how a trust works, and what the legal terms used by trusts mean, it helps to look at how trusts were used in the time of Charles Dickens. Say a wealthy maiden aunt wanted to help a young nephew who was too young to handle money. She would have a *trust deed* drawn up, and the aunt (the *settlor*) would settle or deposit money (the *settled sum*) with a solicitor. The solicitor (the *trustee*) would hold that money in trust on behalf of the nephew (the *beneficiary*), who would benefit from the trust fund after the period of time specified in the trust deed.

Today, discretionary trusts are started by someone, often a family friend, who gives or settles a small sum of money to the trustee to look after. The trustee is given powers in the trust deed to conduct the affairs of the trust and distribute income and capital at his or her discretion to the beneficiaries. This discretionary power to distribute income and capital to the family members who have the lowest rate of tax is what makes a trust such a powerful tax-planning structure.

CHAPTER 2

Getting started: establishing the correct business structure

More mistakes are made at the beginning of a business than at any time in its life. As a result of either not getting advice or receiving the wrong advice, many people end up operating their business through a structure that means they pay too much tax, or that their personal assets are at risk when things go wrong.

When you operate a business, you have the choice of using any of the five main structures available. This chapter looks at what you have to do to prove you are, in fact, running a business, and reviews these five structures.

When a business is not a business

It is important to stress that a choice of business structures is only available when a business is being operated. Where someone is earning 'personal exertion income'—in other words, is really earning employment income—the structures, and thus the tax benefits available, are severely restricted.

There have been many legislative changes over the years to try and curtail the use of tax-effective entities by those earning employment income. Initially, the tax office had to prove that a master/servant relationship existed in order to prove that employment income was being earned—a difficult task. In some early cases the ATO was only successful because the attempt at diverting employment income was so blatant.

A lot of these attempts were labelled 'Friday/Monday schemes'. They involved a person quitting on a Friday as an employee and then turning up for work as a contractor on Monday. Their duties did not change, they still reported to the same person and they still occupied the same office. It will be no surprise that these not-so-cunning schemes (usually attempted so that the person could split income with a non-working spouse) did not succeed.

The next major attempt at attacking tax-effective structures came in the form of part IVA of the tax act. Under this section, the Commissioner of Taxation was given the power to disallow a deduction or arrangement when it could be proven that its prime reason was to reduce tax. Thankfully this section has not been as effective as the commissioner would have liked.

There was a possibility that part IVA would be used to attack a person who changed from a sole trader to a company structure. As it turned out, however, the tax benefits of operating through a company were often minor compared to some of the other benefits—such as the limitation on the owners' legal liability, and the ability to maximise contributions to a super fund. Given these other major benefits, it was almost impossible to apply part IVA.

Recognising that existing measures were not effective, the federal government introduced the 'alienation of personal services income' legislation in 2000. If changes had not been made to this, some couples who were operating a business and taking business risks could have been blocked from receiving tax benefits from any of the legitimate tax structures available.

In its original form, the legislation meant that an entity earning more than 80 per cent of its income from one source could not split that income with anyone in all had to be regarded as income of the person doing the work. Even if less than 80 per cent was earned from one source, other tests had to be satisfied to avoid the imposition of the tax maximising measures of the legislation.

The original wording of the legislation also meant that many people forced to operate a business through a company would have paid a lot more tax. The prime example of this were courier drivers, who had to supply their own vehicles but inevitably were only contracted to one company that found them work. A sufficiently strong case was made on this point that a change was made to protect this group.

The situation now

To prove that you are running a business, and not trying to avoid tax by splitting employment income, there's now a new test that can be used before the 80 per cent test. Under it, a business that earns at least 75 per cent of its income from one source must meet three criteria. The business:

- must be paid to achieve a specified result or outcome, such as cleaning a house, delivering a parcel or installing a kitchen
- must supply plant and equipment or the tools of trade needed to produce the result
- must be required to fix any mistakes or problems that arise from it having carried out the work.

So for example, a husband and wife operating a carpentry contracting business, who supply their own tools and have to fix any defects in the work performed, would pass the test.

If the 80 per cent test is to be applied, after passing it a business must also pass at least one of another three tests. They are:

- that the income was earned from two or more unrelated clients and that the business had offered its services to the general public or a specific section of the public, such as by advertising
- that it operated from business premises that were physically separated from the owners' home or the premises of a client
- that it employed other people or contracted with other entities that earned at least 20 per cent of the business income. In this case, the individuals or entities cannot be associated with the business owner.

In certain circumstances, if a business fails the 80 per cent test, it can apply to have the test waived. The business needs to show it has taken on one long-term contract this year, but had two or more unrelated clients in preceding years. It will also need to show that it's reasonable to expect it will have more than two unrelated clients in the future. Where the business has just started, it will need to show that it reasonably expects to have two or more unrelated clients in the future.

What if you don't pass any of the tests?

If none of the business tests can be satisfied, the trust, company or partnership owning the business does not have to be wound up. The tax deductions allowable will, however, be limited to those that an employed person could get. No deductions will be allowed for rent, mortgage interest, home to work travel or wages paid to an associated person or relative who does not earn the income. The only time home to work travel will be deductible is where the vehicle is used to transport bulky equipment.

A business that fails the tests can however claim deductions for expenses that strictly relate to the income earned. These include advertising for work, income protection and public liability insurance, workers compensation insurance, contracting with an independent person or entity, superannuation for the person actually earning the income, registration and company fees, and cars used for business purposes. The rules also allow for one private car to be claimed using the fringe benefits tax system by a business that failed the test.

When the business is a business, but making a loss

Once it's been established that a business is being operated, one of the benefits is to be able to offset business losses against other income. But before this can be done the business must be able to pass one of the following non-commercial business loss tests:

- generate income of at least $20 000 in a full year, or
- use real property, such as real estate valued at no less than $500 000, or
- use other assets such as plant and equipment, stock and leased assets valued at least $100 000, or

- have produced a profit in at least three of the previous five years.

If none of the tests can be passed (and the last test is impossible for start-up businesses to pass), an application can be made to the ATO for the non-commercial business loss provisions to be waived. To be successful in this, a business plan should be prepared that includes profit and cash-flow projections that predict how long it will take for the business to become profitable.

Choosing a business structure

Once it's been established that a business is being operated, or going to be operated, a person can choose any of the different business structures available. These are:

- sole trader
- partnership
- discretionary family trust
- unit trust
- company
- partnership of discretionary trusts.

As mentioned earlier, the type of tax structure you operate a business through can have far-reaching ramifications if you get it wrong. The consequences can include paying too much income tax, putting your personal assets at risk, paying too much capital gains tax or missing out on generous tax concessions on the sale of goodwill.

Most businesses go through several stages of development. This is more apparent when they're started from scratch, but it can also apply when a business is purchased as a going concern. Depending on the stage that your business is at, you may have different requirements. Fortunately, from an income tax point of view there's nothing to stop you operating a business initially through one structure, such as a sole trader, then at a later stage changing to a structure that meets your needs better. The ATO will not be able to challenge this change in business structure, as long as the prime reason for changing was not to obtain a tax benefit. When it comes to choosing a business structure, however, income tax should only be one of many considerations taken into account. And if you consider these other factors, the chance of the ATO successfully attacking any change in structure is greatly reduced.

Sole trader

The sole trader structure is the most common one used by those starting a business. When the business is being started on a part-time basis while the owner continues in full-time employment, having a sole trader structure can reduce his or her tax payable on the employment income if losses are made. (Of course, this tax reduction is subject to the business satisfying the non-commercial business loss provisions previously mentioned.)

This income tax advantage becomes a disadvantage when the business starts to make profits, as the business income will be added to the owner's employment income. This could mean that tax is paid at the higher tax rates of 40 per cent and 45 per cent when the total income exceeds the relevant thresholds.

Compared to the other business structures, operating as a sole trader is the cheapest option to set up—there are no set-up costs unless a business name is required. In addition, the only administration needed is an accounting or book-keeping system that produces a statement showing the total business revenue and expenses and the amount of profit or loss made.

Capital gains tax is not a major issue for someone operating as a sole trader, either. The general 50 per cent capital gains tax exemption is available to individual taxpayers, and after also applying the 50 per cent active assets exemption available to qualifying small business owners, only 25 per cent of a capital gain on the sale of a business is assessable. In addition, if the resulting capital gain is rolled into a super fund, the business would have to be sold for over $2 million in profit before tax would be payable.

Legal liability and protection of personal assets are two other areas in which sole traders are at a major disadvantage. If the business is subjected to a legal claim, and insurance does not cover the full extent of any damages awarded, the owner's personal assets can be used to pay the damages. However, this is really only a big consideration if the business has a high level of operational risk—a tree-felling business, for example. In the event of a tree falling the wrong way and destroying a house, the business owner may be forced to sell his or her own home to pay for rebuilding that house.

Another risk can arise if a sole trader incurs large debts to suppliers then fails: the suppliers can attack the owner's personal assets to meet any shortfall owed by the business. If they are married, one way sole traders can protect themselves against this happening is to have all of their personal assets owned by their spouse.

As people cannot employ themselves, sole traders are not required to pay WorkCover on the earnings they make from the business. This however also means that if an accident occurs they will not receive WorkCover benefits. To protect themselves, sole traders should take out income protection insurance.

Given the pros and cons, operating as a sole trader is best suited to a person who does not have any family members to split business profits with and operates a business that has a low level of legal risk. It is also a good way of operating when a business is being developed and losses are being incurred. Of course, once profits are generated, or the threat of legal liability becomes a problem, there is no reason why a change cannot be made to one of the other entities.

Partnerships

Partnerships are one of the simplest and most common forms of tax structure used other than the sole trader structure. A partnership as an entity does not pay tax: any profits the business makes are distributed to the partners, and tax is paid at their applicable tax rate. It's often not understood, however, that tax must be paid on a partner's share of profits, not on the amount of cash he or she has withdrawn from the business.

Likewise, the amount of loss that can be offset against a partner's other sources of income is his or her share of the partnership loss, not the amount of money he or she contributed to the partnership. The ability to distribute losses can be a tax benefit in the set up stage of a business the same as it is for a sole trader.

For example, Bud is a 50 per cent partner with Lou in an entertainment business that has been experiencing cash flow problems in the 2008 year, and deposited $10 000 in that year to help it out. Due to some of the money being used for non-deductible outgoings, such as loan payments, the loss in that year was only $8000. Bud can only claim his share of the $8000 loss.

This benefit extends to allowing partners to decrease employment income when commercial business losses are made. Let's say Bud worked part time to earn money to help while the business was still being established. The income from his job for 2008 was $25 000. This means if his share of the loss is $4000 he can decrease his employment income by $4000.

Also, depending on the partnership agreement, a partner working outside the business can be given the tax benefit of all or most of a business loss made. The agreement must recognise that the partner working in the business should be compensated for having done most of the work. As a result, the business loss claimable by that partner decreases, and increases correspondingly for the partner working elsewhere.

There is however a downside to being able to claim losses. When the business becomes profitable income can only be split between the partners. This can result in income tax being paid at the top marginal rate.

Partnership can be the next most cost-effective tax structure to set up after a sole trader. Apart from the cost of registering a business name, the only expense is drawing up the partnership agreement. This cost can vary from as little as $30 for an off-the-shelf agreement to over $1000 for a detailed agreement drawn up by a solicitor.

Often when people operate as a partnership, particularly husbands and wives, a formal partnership agreement is not drawn up. However, where non-related parties go into partnership it is vital that an agreement is prepared. In the event of a partnership dispute, the money saved by not having an agreement will soon be eaten up with legal costs to resolve the dispute.

At a minimum, an agreement should cover:

- what each partner is contributing to the business, either in the form of equipment or money
- how the profits are to be split
- the frequency and amount of cash drawings
- what work is expected to be performed by each partner.

This last point is one of the most common reasons why partnerships involving unrelated parties fail. Agreement should be reached at the start about how many hours each partner is expected to work, and how a partner who works extra hours will be rewarded for the extra effort. If this has not been agreed the chances of a dispute arising and the partnership splitting up are higher.

Operating through a partnership has a capital gains tax benefit as well as an income tax benefit. As the individuals in the partnership pay tax on capital gains made, they receive the general 50 per cent CGT discount. Where the gain is made on the sale of the business, and they pass the relevant tests, they also receive the 50 per cent active assets discount. This can mean that if a husband and wife who sell their business for a $4 million capital gain each contribute $500 000 of the gain into a super fund, they will not pay any capital gains tax.

In addition to their other advantages, partnerships do not require complicated administration systems. There only needs to be a simple bookkeeping system that allows the partnership to keep track of how much income it earns, what its expenses are, and how much each partner is owed or owes the partnership, as shown in their equity account. Equity accounts are affected by profits distributed, capital contributed, losses made and drawings taken.

Drawings can be a major source of confusion for partners. There is a common misconception that money taken out as drawings from a partnership is counted as taxable income for the partner. This is not the case. It is the only partner's share of the business profit that determines his or her tax liability and not how much money they take out as drawings.

To illustrate this, let's assume that in the 2009 year Bud and Lou's entertainment business really took off, and after all expenses the partnership made a profit of $80 000. The cash flow during this year was so good that Bud was able to withdraw cash of $50 000 to help pay his personal expenses. Nevertheless, for 2009 Bud only counts his share of the profit ($40 000) as taxable income, not the $50 000 he withdrew.

Two of the biggest disadvantages with operating as a partnership are the protection of personal assets and legal liability. Under partnership law, each partner is jointly and severally liable for the debts of the partnership. So, in the event of the business failing, or a claim for damages against the business not being covered by its assets, the personal assets of the partners can be used to meet the debts of the partnership.

When a business fails, partners may bear the financial burden unequally. If one partner has assets outside the business, such as a family home, and the other partner has very little, the partner with the assets can end up paying all the business's debts.

Another disadvantage of a partnership is that the partners, like sole traders, cannot cover themselves using WorkCover insurance. They should consider taking out income protection insurance.

Unit trusts

Unit trusts are not used very often, but they work in very much the same way as companies, except that units are issued instead of shares. The only major difference is in the tax treatment of their profits. Companies are taxed entities, and tax is paid on profits at the company rate of 30 per cent. Unit trusts, by contrast, do not have their profits taxed. Instead, the profit is distributed each year to the unitholders in the proportion the units are held, and each unitholder pays the tax. Note however that some unit trust deeds allow profits to be distributed in accordance with an agreement signed by all unit holders, instead of strictly in proportion to the units held by each person. This adds some degree of flexibility to unit trusts.

A trust is not recognised as a legal entity; everything owned by a trust is owned in the name of the trustee, which is responsible for the day-to-day operations of the trust. The trustee can be one person or a number of people; it can also be a company. One point to note is that where individuals are trustees, they can become personally responsible for the debts of the unit trust—so if legal liability is a problem for your business, you may wish to have a company act as trustee.

The cost of setting up a unit trust depends on whether individuals or a company are going to be the trustees. Where individuals are the trustees, it can cost from $400 up to more than $1000, depending on who you use and how complicated the trust deed is. Where a company will be acting as trustee, the set-up cost increases by approximately $1100 to between $1500 and $2100.

Unlike companies, the general 50 per cent capital gains tax discount is available to the owners of the units if they are individuals. Where a company owns the units, this discount is lost.

The biggest disadvantage of using a unit trust relates to the small business CGT exemptions. A unit trust that passes the various tests can use the 50 per cent active asset exemption, but no real benefit is obtained by its unitholders. This is because if the discount is retained within the trust it is taxed at the top tax rate, and if it is distributed as a non-taxable distribution, it decreases the original purchase cost of the units. This has the effect of increasing the capital gain made when the units are eventually sold or the trust is wound up.

For example, say Jerry and Dean operate their accounting business through a unit trust, and when they set up the business they each purchased $100 000 of units. They sell a business property and make a capital gain of $100 000 that qualifies for the 50 per cent active asset exemption. If they claim the exemption and distribute the non-taxable $50 000, the cost of their units will be only $75 000, not the original $100 000.

Another disadvantage is that according to the relevant legislation, where individuals act as trustees they cannot employ themselves. This means they cannot pay themselves a wage under the PAYG system or take out workers compensation insurance, and should think about taking out income protection insurance instead.

Discretionary family trusts

There is a general principle that you have to spend money to make money. When it comes to tax structures, the principle becomes, 'The more complicated and costly the structure, the more tax-effective it will be'. Operating as a sole trader is the simplest and cheapest structure, and can be the least tax-effective. A discretionary family trust is one of the most complicated and costly structures, but is the most flexible and tax-effective.

A family trust is the most tax-effective structure to operate a business through because it enables the business profit to be distributed among the family members. The profit can be distributed to family members with the lowest income, so that tax is paid at the lower tax rates for each individual family member. In some circumstances, a trust can distribute income to a company, so that after-tax profits can be maximised to fund growth of the business.

Let's look at an example. Ron operates a public relations business through a family trust. He wins a contract to improve the image of politicians that is success-based — to get the maximum amount of money from the contract, he has to improve the rating of the politicians. Through a campaign based around the cream of Australia's sporting heroes, he lifts their popularity rating several places, from being at the bottom to being just ahead of used-car salesmen.

The bonus he earns in the 2008 year is $200 000, and Ron wants to use this money to help grow his business and open offices in the other states. His trust does not have a company as a beneficiary, and after taking into account the salary he received pays tax at the top rate on $100 000. This leaves him with $53 500 after tax to fund the set-up of the new offices. If he had a company beneficiary, he would have distributed $100 000 to it, leaving the business with $70 000 in after-tax funds.

The amount of tax saved by distributing to family members will depend on how many are over 18 or working full-time in the business. A family with a husband and wife and two children under the age of 18 will mean a trust is only marginally more tax-effective than a partnership. This is because non-working children under 18 for the 2008 year can only receive approximately $1300 before they start paying tax, and income distributed above this will be taxed at the top marginal tax rate or even more.

If the children in the family are over 18 and not working, however (possibly because they are still attending school or university), a trust is much more tax-effective than a partnership. For example, a trust in this situation that makes a business profit of $208 000, including wages paid to the owners, would pay tax at the 15 per cent and 30 per cent rates if it had the two parents and two student beneficiaries over the age of 18 to distribute to. As the 30 per cent tax rate is payable on income up to $75 000, tax is not paid at more than this rate. If a husband-and-wife partnership operated the same business, tax would be paid on most of the profit at the 30 per cent rate, with some at the 40 per cent rate.

When a trustee distributes income to a beneficiary, it does not have to physically pay him or her the money. Often, the trustee simply draws up a minute that states how much of each year's profit is distributed to each of the beneficiaries. These distributions are recorded in the books of the trust as amounts owed. Whenever amounts are actually paid to or on behalf of each beneficiary, the amount of money owed to them by the trust reduces.

There is a risk attached to distributing income in this way to children. When no amounts are actually paid to them, or they are not recorded properly, a large debt to the children can build up, and in the event of a family dispute, major financial problems can be created for the business if the children demand that that debt be repaid.

To ensure that the debt does not become too large, costs relating to the children (such as education fees, holidays, tax on income distributed to them and car expenses) should be paid by the trust instead of the parents. In this way, the loan owing to each of the children will not keep increasing, and there may even be a situation where money is owed back to the trust by the children.

As it is the individual beneficiaries of a trust that pay tax on the income distributed to them, all of the CGT benefits are available to a trust. The beneficiaries of a trust get this benefit, plus, as long as the significant individual test is passed, all of the small business CGT concessions.

The cost of setting up a trust depends on who the trustee is. Where an individual is the trustee, the cost will be approximately $400, and this will cover the cost of drawing up the trust deed and the government fees that apply.

As with unit trusts, where protection of a business owner's assets is important a company should act as trustee. All activities of a trust are carried on by, and in the name of, the trustee, so if a business fails, or there is a legal claim against the business, the trustee's assets are at risk. Having a $2 company act as trustee means the assets of the real owners are not at risk — but the set-up costs increase. The cost of the company is approximately $1100.

Still, that can be money very well spent. A client I had operated a building business through a trust that he was the trustee of. A boy went onto one of its building sites, and while playing had an accident that left him with brain injuries. Despite the business having all of the required fencing and other safety equipment in place, the parents of the boy successfully sued the trust and won damages of $1.5 million. The trust's insurance cover was only $1 million, and this left my client facing a personal debt of $500 000 because he was the trustee. If he'd had a $2 company acting as trustee, he would not have been liable for the shortfall.

However, having a company act as trustee will not protect the assets of the business owners when they are the directors, in some cases. If it can be proved that they incurred debts on behalf of the trust knowing they could not be paid, they could be held responsible for those debts.

Where a trust has individuals acting as trustees, they cannot theoretically employ themselves, in much the same way as partners cannot employ themselves. This means that where the owners are also the trustees, they cannot make super contributions as employees and cannot be covered by WorkCover insurance. If a company acts as trustee, of course, the owners can employ themselves and make super contributions up to the relevant maximum limit.

Trusts with individual trustees require more administration than sole traders or partnerships. Trusts with a company acting as trustee are the most complicated and costly to administer, as they have the administration both of the trust and of the company to attend to.

Companies

Over recent years, companies have become a very popular way of owning and operating a business, and many people have been drawn to the company structure in the mistaken belief that they would pay less tax. The truth is companies at best delay paying tax, and at worst they can mean more capital gains tax is paid than necessary.

One major area in which companies do have an advantage over other business structures is when unrelated parties want to own a business together. Unlike a partnership, which must cease when partners enter or leave the business, companies continue no matter how often ownership of the shares change. A company is also the only structure to have if a person wants to grow the business to the point of listing it on the stock exchange.

Because a company is regarded as a separate legal entity, the assets of the owners are not at risk if the company fails due to unprofitable trading or because of a legal claim. The only times when shareholders' assets can be at risk are:

- when they are also directors and they have given personal guarantees, or
- where the tax office has issued a notice to the directors stating that they will be personally liable for PAYG withholding tax owing, or
- it can be proven they incurred debts in the name of the company and knew the company could not repay the debt.

Being regarded as a separate legal entity also means the company can employ the owners. This means the owners have the benefit of being covered by WorkCover insurance, which could be cheaper than income protection insurance, depending on their age. In addition, they can have super contributions made for them up to the limit, and the business can pay for a private car using the fringe benefits tax system.

The company tax rate of 30 per cent does have a benefit, too, for business owners wanting to invest after-tax profits back into a business. Compared with the other tax structures such as partnerships and trusts, where tax can be paid at 45 per cent, a company can allow more profit to be retained to build the business as was explained in Ron's example in the previous section. However, when owners want to spend their profits they must get it out in the form of wages, dividends or loans.

When wages and fully franked dividends are paid to shareholders, tax is paid at the relevant tax rate. Depending on their income from other sources, this can mean they will pay tax on the profit at the top tax rate. Where loans are taken by shareholders, interest must be charged by the company and the loans must be repaid in at least seven years. If this is not done, the amount taken can be classed as an unfranked dividend. If the loan is, however, repaid with franked dividends over the seven years, shareholders will eventually pay tax at their normal tax rate but receive the 30 per cent franking credit.

Being able to pay tax at the company rate then distribute dividends over time can be a benefit for a business that experiences fluctuating levels of profit. Where such a business is owned by a sole trader, partnership or most trusts, tax may be paid in some years at the lowest rate of 15 per cent, while in other years it can be 45 per cent.

However, companies are at a major disadvantage when it comes to set-up costs and ease of administration. The cost of setting up a company can range from $900 up to more than $1500. In addition, companies cost more to maintain, as a $212 fee must be paid to the Australian Securities & Investments Commission (ASIC) each year.

Companies also require more administration and recordkeeping. As well as maintaining normal bookkeeping and accounting records, a company must maintain a register of its shareholders and officers. In addition, in a company, decisions should be made by meetings of directors that need to be documented in the form of minutes. All this extra administration translates into increased accounting costs of approximately $300 per year.

By far the greatest disadvantage of operating through a company is the way capital gains tax is calculated. Under the changes introduced in 1999, companies do not receive the general 50 per cent discount. Where a company owns an asset and the capital profit is distributed to the shareholder, tax could be paid at 46.5 per cent, whereas when individuals on the top rate make a capital gain, they pay 23.25 per cent on it.

Companies don't just miss out on the general discount — there is another capital gains benefit that does not apply, and that is the 50 per cent discount applied to active assets such as goodwill or a business property. Although the company's significant shareholders do get the concession, the 50 per cent discount of the capital gain must be paid out as an unfranked dividend.

When this untaxed gain is distributed as an unfranked dividend, tax is paid on all of the gain at the marginal tax rate of the shareholders. At best, if this accumulated profit is distributed to shareholders when the company is wound up they can get the 50 per cent general discount, but they pay tax on this at their applicable tax rate.

The impact of this is best illustrated by an example. Say a business is sold for a profit on goodwill of $900 000. If the business was owned by a partnership of six individuals, the profit would be decreased by the 50 per cent general exemption and the 50 per cent active assets exemption. The partners could contribute $37500 each of the assessable profit to a super fund, so no tax would be payable under the retirement exemption.

If that same business was owned through a company by the six individuals equally, tax would be paid by the company of $270000, 30 per cent of the $900000, as no CGT small business concessions could be used. If only four shareholders under 55 owned the company equally, $900000 would have to be contributed to a super fund to claim the retirement exemption. If they claimed the active asset discount, that would leave $450000 in the company as untaxed profit, and that would have tax paid on it when taken by the shareholders.

For a more complete explanation of the capital gains rules, refer to chapter 12, 'Minimising tax on selling a business'.

A partnership of trusts

Where unrelated parties own a business, the most flexible structure is a partnership of trusts. This means each owner has a trust to own the business. For this structure to be able to provide maximum tax and legal liability benefits, the partnership would be made up as follows:

- *Company acting as nominee for the partnership of trusts.*
  The ownership of the nominee company would
  reflect the ownership of the business. Decisions of the
  partnership would be made in line with decisions made
  by the board of directors of the nominee company.

- *Two or more trusts are the actual owners of the business
  through a partnership.* Discretionary trusts would be

formed to be the actual owners of the business, with a partnership agreement being drawn up to reflect this fact. The agreement could allow for profits to be split in accordance with stated percentages, and also for unequal distributions if all partners agreed to them in writing.

- *Each trust would have a separate company acting as trustee.* To ensure the individual owners are protected, companies would act as trustee for each of the trusts. The trust deeds would need to allow for profits to be distributed to these trustee companies. This set-up can save tax if the individual owners would pay tax at a higher rate than the company one — thus, more of the profits can be retained to build the business.

- *Other assets and investments would be owned by totally separate trusts.* This final step is only necessary if the owners of the business have substantial other assets and investments they want to protect in the event of a legal claim that results from the operations of the business.

A partnership of trusts is by far the most costly structure to set up, but provides the maximum opportunity to save both income tax and capital gains tax, allows for flexibility, and provides a high degree of legal protection for the owners. One downside of the structure, however, is that if partners want to join or leave it a whole new partnership needs to be formed.

You can see from this chapter that there are a lot of things to consider when deciding what structure to use for a business. To make sure you make the right choice, seek the advice of an accountant who specialises in the area.

CHAPTER 3

The Small Business Entities Simplified Tax System

Prior to 1 July 2007, the Simplified Tax System (STS) provided tax benefits to businesses that passed certain tests. The problem with this old system was that its tests were complicated and in most cases businesses had to accept all of the concessions, whether they wanted them or not. (For example, because the STS depreciation rates in some cases do not produce as big a deduction.) For the 2007–08 year and all subsequent years the STS has been replaced by the Small Business Entities Tax System (SBE system).

Do you qualify as a small business entity?

To qualify as a small business entity, you must be carrying on a business and earn less than $2 million in annual turnover. However, as you would expect with anything to do with income tax, this turnover test is actually three tests, not one. Before I explain further, you first need to understand that it is the *aggregated turnover* of a business that is counted.

Although the new SBE system is less complicated than STS, those wonderful drafters of tax legislation in Treasury could not help themselves. What follows is the legislation detailing what aggregated turnover does not include:

328-115(3) Your *aggregated turnover* for an income year does not include the following amounts:

(a) amounts derived in the income year by you or a relevant entity from dealings between you and the relevant entity while the relevant entity is connected with you or is your affiliate;

(b) amounts derived in the income year by a relevant entity from dealings between the relevant entity and another relevant entity while each relevant entity is connected with you or is your affiliate;

(c) amounts derived in the income year by a relevant entity while the relevant entity is not connected with you and is not your affiliate.

The stuff these guys come up with is mind-boggling!

An experience I had on one of my many visits to Canberra for a Federal Budget might help explain why tax legislation can be so incomprehensible. It was during the time of the Hawke Labor Government, and there was a new piece of tax legislation being introduced that I could not make sense of. When I approached a Treasury official for an explanation, his reply went something like this: 'Don't ask me what it means, we only write the stuff. It's up to the tax office to make sense of it'.

To understand what tax legislation means, it sometimes helps to first work out what it's attempting to achieve. All this talk of connected entities and affiliates is designed to stop people from getting under the $2 million turnover threshold by having different business entities. So, if you own several companies, or through some other relationship can be said to exercise some control over other businesses, the turnover of those businesses plus yours must be aggregated, or added together, when calculating the turnover for the test.

You, however, do not have to include any sales or income from transactions *between* these entities, only the sales or turnover on transactions with third parties. For most people, fortunately, the turnover counted is the total revenue for just their business—nice and simple.

The three qualifying tests

To qualify for the SBE system, you only have to pass one of three tests based on different time periods. To pass the first test, your aggregate turnover for the previous year must be less than $2 million. It does not matter if your income in the year you are using the SBE system exceeds the $2 million, just as long as the turnover for the previous year was less than the limit.

If for some reason you cannot pass this test, you may be able to pass the second test. You pass this test if, on the first day of the financial year in question, you estimate that the turnover for your business is likely to be less than $2 million for that year. You can take into account such things as changes in business conditions, the loss of contracts, or even the impact of drought or other things that affect your turnover. However, you cannot use this test if your income exceeded the $2 million limit in both of the two previous years.

If you fail the first two tests, you can still qualify for the SBE under the third test—your actual turnover for the year must less than the $2 million. But because this test, of course, can only be satisfied after the year has ended, you do not get the GST concessions or the benefit of paying estimated PAYG instalments.

For an example of how these tests work, let's look at a company we'll call Brian's Bin Hire. In the 2006 and 2007 financial years, its total income from bin hire exceeded $2 million each year. This made Brian's business ineligible for the SBE concessions at the start of the 2008 year. The turnover for 2008, however, ended up being $1.9 million, so Brian can apply to be in the SBE for the 2008 and the 2009 years.

Note that once the business is in the SBE system, it can be forced out if it no longer meets the eligibility criteria. A taxpayer can also choose to leave the SBE — in which case, he or she must wait at least five years before choosing to use the depreciation concessions again. All the other concessions can be used again sooner if the business qualifies for them.

The concessions

A business that qualifies as an SBE applies for each concession it wishes to take advantage of by completing the relevant forms. The benefits available are:

- four capital gains tax concessions:
    * the CGT 15-year asset exemption
    * the CGT 50 per cent active asset reduction
    * the CGT retirement exemption
    * the CGT rollover
- simpler depreciation rules
- simpler trading stock rules
- entrepreneurs' tax offset
- an FBT car-parking exemption
- being able to deduct certain prepaid business expenses immediately
- being able to account for GST on a cash basis

- being able to pay GST by quarterly instalments
- being able to apportion GST input tax credits annually
- that your PAYG instalments are based on GDP-adjusted notional tax
- having a two-year period in which you can amend assessments.

Let's look at these benefits in a little more detail.

Capital gains tax concessions

One of the big changes brought in by the SBE system was the creation of a link with the capital gains tax concessions that previously did not exist. I will not provide a full explanation of how the four CGT concessions work here: this is covered in chapter 12, 'Minimising tax on selling a business'. The main point to make is that in order to be eligible for the CGT concessions, the business must be a small business entity. Where business owners qualify as an SBE entity, they can have assets of more than $6 million (including the value of their business), and still qualify for the CGT concessions. If they are not in the SBE system, they will not qualify for these concessions if the net value of their assets exceeds $6 million.

Simpler depreciation rules

Under the SBE system the calculation of depreciating assets is not only simpler, but the tax deduction is often increased. Instead of working out the effective useful life of each asset, and writing it off over that period, depreciating assets are split into three broad categories:

- Assets costing less than $1000. These can be written off in full in the year they are purchased.
- All other depreciating assets are split into two pools:
  * Those that have a useful life of less than 25 years are in the general pool, and are depreciated at the rate of 30 per cent per year.
  * Those with a life of greater than 25 years are in the long-life pool, and are depreciated at the rate of 5 per cent per year.

Under normal depreciation rules, an asset purchased during the year must have the claim for depreciation pro-rated over the period of the financial year it was owned. Under the SBE rules, an asset purchased during the year is depreciated as though it was purchased halfway through the year. As a result, assets purchased during the year are written off at 15 per cent if they are in the general pool and 2.5 per cent if they are in the long-life pool.

When assets that were included in one of the two pools are sold, the sale proceeds are deducted from the opening balance of the relevant pool. This means the closing value of an asset in the general pool is calculated in table 3.1, overleaf.

If the balance of a pool is less than $1000 after the proceeds from the sale of assets have been deducted, the value of the pool can be written off in full. Where the balance of the pool is a minus figure, after deducting sale proceeds, this value is included as assessable income for the year.

Say that James has a mowing business. He has been using the STS depreciation system for a number of years; at the start of the 2008 year he qualifies for the SBE system and has general pool assets of $3000. He buys a new ride-on mower for $4500 during the year, and purchases a new van using lease finance, receiving $6800 as a trade-in on his old van. Taking into account these transactions, the value of his general pool is $700.

As the balance of the pool is less than $1000, the full $700 can be written off and the closing balance for the general pool will be zero. If James had received $8000 as a trade-in, though, the negative $500 balance of his general pool would have had to be included as income for the 2008 year.

When a business opts out of the SBE system, or no longer meets the eligibility criteria, it can continue to deduct the cost of the assets in each of the pools, but cannot add any further assets to the pools.

Table 3.1: calculating a general pool asset's closing value

Opening balance

PLUS

Assets purchased during the year over $1000

LESS

Proceeds from the sale of assets in the pool during the year

LESS

Depreciation at 30 per cent of the opening balance

LESS

Depreciation at 15 per cent of new assets
purchased during the year

EQUALS

Closing balance for the pool

Simpler trading stock rules

If there is likely to be a difference of less than $5000 between the opening and the closing stock figures of a business in the SBE system, the business only has to make a reasonable estimate of the quantity and value of the stock each year, instead of counting it accurately. A record should be kept of how the estimate was made.

Be warned, however: not having to count stock accurately simplifies things, but it can also be a trap—often when stock is not accurately counted on a regular basis, stock losses cannot be detected. In addition, unless you accurately measure the stock on hand, you can never really know how profitable your business is.

The entrepreneurs' tax offset

To be eligible for the entrepreneurs' tax offset, the total annual aggregated turnover of your business cannot be more than $75000, and the business must have produced 'net small business income' (net profit) for the year. 'Aggregated turnover' is the total turnover for the business—in the case of a partner it is the partnership's aggregated total turnover; for a beneficiary it is the trust's aggregated turnover of the trust.

The full 25 per cent offset is available to individuals, trustees and companies with aggregated 'net small business income' of up to $50000. It then phases out until you reach $75000 in income.

Table 3.2, overleaf, shows how the offset is calculated.

Table 3.2: calculating the entrepreneurs' tax offset

Step 1   Calculate your taxable income for the year.

Step 2   Calculate the tax payable on your taxable income.

Step 3   Multiply the tax payable by 25 per cent.

Step 4   Calculate the percentage your business income is of your taxable income.

Step 5   If your aggregated turnover is $50 000 or less, multiply the amount calculated at step 3 by the percentage from step 4. This is your offset.

If your aggregated turnover is more than $50 000 you calculate your 'small business phase-out fraction' — subtract your aggregated turnover from $75 000, then divide this amount by $25 000. The offset is then calculated by multiplying the amount calculated at step 3 by the percentage from step 4, then multiplying this by your 'small business phase-out fraction'.

How the offset works is best explained by the following two examples. Say that Packer Pty Ltd produces a small publication aimed at the gambling industry. For the 2008 year, it has an annual turnover of $60 000 and, as there are no other businesses associated or connected with it, its aggregated turnover is also $60 000. It has no other income and makes a net profit for the year of $10 000. The offset is calculated in table 3.3.

William Gates operates a small computer consultancy business. He advertises in the local paper and has four customers that he looks after. In addition to running his business, he has a part-time job in the local supermarket. For the 2008 year his business has a turnover of $40 000 and after costs makes a profit of $30 000. His only other income for the year was $20 000 in wages from his part-time job, giving him a taxable income of $50 000. His offset is calculated in table 3.4.

Table 3.3: Packer Pty Ltd's offset

Step 1	Taxable income	$10 000
Step 2	Tax payable	$3 000
Step 3	Full potential offset	$750
Step 4	Business income as a percentage of taxable income	100 per cent
Step 5	Aggregated income is more than $50 000, so:	
	$75 000 − $60 000 =	$15 000
	$15 000 ÷ $25 000	60 per cent
	Offset = $750 x 100 per cent x 60 per cent	$450

Table 3.4: William Gates's offset

Step 1	Taxable income	$50 000
Step 2	Tax payable	$9 600
Step 3	Full potential offset	$2 400
Step 4	Business income as a percentage of taxable income	60 per cent
Step 5	Aggregated income is less than $50 000, so:	
	Offset = $2400 x 60 per cent	$1 440

Fringe benefits tax car-parking exemption

Non-SBE businesses must pay fringe benefits tax on any car parking provided to their employees if there is a commercial car park within one kilometre of the business premises. An SBE business, however, is exempt from this fringe benefits tax. For the concession to apply, the car park must be at the businesses premises and the car must not be parked at a commercial car park.

Deducting prepaid expenses immediately

Electing to be covered by SBE allows a business to claim a tax deduction immediately for certain prepaid expenses. The prepayment rules do not apply, however, to amounts paid:

- of less than $1000
- that were required by law or as a result of a court order
- for salary and wages, including superannuation
- that are private or domestic in nature or are of a capital nature, such as new plant and equipment.

In order to be claimed as a prepaid expense, the services must be for a period of not more than 12 months, and must expire in the next income year. Businesses not using the SBE system are unable to claim a deduction for services that will be provided in a future tax year.

Here's an example of how this works. Say Machine Sales Pty Ltd makes a big sale in May 2008. Their turnover is still less than $2 million for the 2008 year, but their net profit has increased by $50 000. If it does nothing, the company will be paying $15 000 in tax on the extra profit.

The company rents its business premises for $40 000 a year, so it decides to prepay the rent on 1 June 2008 for the next 12 months. As the rental payment is not for more than 12 months and the prepayment period runs out in the 2009 tax year, Machine Sales can claim the full $40 000 against its 2008 profit. This will reduce its tax payable for 2008 by $12 000, and will also improve its cash flow for the 2009 year, as it won't have to pay rent again until June 2009.

If the company prepaid its rent for three years, the payment would have to be apportioned on a days' basis over the three years the payment related to. This would result in no decrease in tax for the 2008 year.

Accounting for GST using the cash method

Most businesses are required to use the accrual method of accounting for income tax purposes. Under that method, income is taxable when it is earned, and costs are deductible when they are owed — rather than when they are paid. This means that a business can pay tax on income that it is owed but has not yet collected.

It also means that businesses must pay GST to the ATO on income they have earned but not yet collected — fortunately, they can also claim GST input tax credits on amounts they owe but have not yet paid.

Business in the SBE system, however, can elect to pay their GST on a cash basis. In other words, they only have to send the GST they've actually collected to the ATO — and they can only claim GST input tax credits on amounts they've actually paid.

Paying GST in quarterly instalments

Most businesses account for GST on either a monthly or quarterly basis using the actual method, which involves accounting for the GST collected and the GST input tax credits received constantly over a month or a quarter. The business activity statements (BAS) lodged by these businesses show the actual amounts of GST collected and paid.

By contrast, an SBE business can instead choose to pay a quarterly GST instalment amount calculated by the ATO. The business then lodges an annual GST statement that has all the actual figures on it. This concession can be a mixed blessing as you can end up with a large GST bill if the quarterly instalments payments are less than what turns out to be actually owed at the end of the year. Of course, you could also end up with a refund if the instalments were too high.

Apportioning GST credits annually

In normal circumstances, a business can only claim a GST input tax credit on business expenses. This means that if you purchase an item for both business and private use (a car, say), you can only claim the business-use portion of the GST paid.

Businesses in the SBE system can choose to account for the private-use portion of such purchases or payments annually. They claim the full amount of the GST paid every quarter or month, and then adjust a future BAS to take into account the GST relating to private use. This means instead of calculating the private use GST component every month or quarter it only has to be done once a year.

PAYG instalments using the GDP amount

PAYG instalments are paid by taxpayers who earn business or investment income, as opposed to employment income. Normally PAYG instalments are calculated by multiplying the actual assessable income for the month or quarter by an instalment rate notified by the ATO. A taxpayer in the SBE system, however, can choose to pay its PAYG instalments quarterly based on a notional GDP-adjusted quarterly instalment amount provided by the ATO. This can mean if the quarterly amounts are too low, and the taxpayer has not put away funds to pay the tax, they can experience cash flow problems.

A two-year period for amending assessments

If a business is not an SBE, the ATO can amend a tax assessment up to four years after it was issued. In other words, the ATO has up to four years to audit a business or discover any mistakes, during which time it can amend the tax assessment and demand extra tax if necessary.

For SBE businesses, the ATO can only amend assessments going back two years. Of course, if it can prove that a business has been involved in tax avoidance, fraud or evasion, no time limit applies!

CHAPTER 4

Income tax

It's not important for a business owner to have detailed knowledge of taxation law, but not having at least a basic understanding is like playing a game without knowing the rules! Ignorance is not bliss. Players who don't know the rules eventually make a mistake and are penalised in some way, and if the mistake is bad enough they can even lose the game.

Paying more tax

Before I get into explaining some of the broader tax concepts, it is important that I make a statement that may have you questioning my sanity. It's this: my hope is that you will be paying the maximum amount of tax that you can.

Let me qualify that. After you've organised yourself in the most tax-effective way and taken advantage of all the sensible tax deductions you can (including tax-effective investments), I hope you're paying a lot of tax. Because if you are in this enviable situation, you must be making LOTS OF MONEY.

During the 30-plus years I have been advising small business owners on business and tax issues, clients have often said two things to me that do not make a lot of sense, and reveal a nonsensical and unhealthy attitude to tax. The first is, 'How can I maximise my tax deduction?' This is often asked when a client needs help making a decision on something like buying a new vehicle. The second is, 'Why would I do that? I'll only be paying more tax.' This is usually said after I have given the client a tip on how to make more money, such as shifting excess cash from a cheque account into a cash management account.

When I'm presented with these irrational statements, I like to provide my clients with an alternative. I offer to give them an invoice for, say, $10 000 of accounting services that will be 100 per cent tax-deductible. I then explain that once they've paid me and secured the tax deduction, I'll happily assume the tax obligation on their behalf. The funny thing is, not one client has yet taken up my extremely generous offer.

One of the golden rules for business should be: 'Never do something purely for tax reasons: make the best business decision that you can make first, then decide on the most tax-effective way of implementing that decision.'

For example, say Joe owns a construction business. The building boom has been good to him and he decides that his 10-year-old ute is costing too much and should be updated. He is facing a big tax bill this year, and if he bought a $150 000 Mercedes ute it would give him a huge tax deduction. However, he works out that all he really needs is another four-wheel drive ute, and decides that a Toyota HiLux Dual Cab diesel, costing $48 000, will give him what he wants at the best price he can find. So, after checking with his accountant, he buys the car in May 2008 using lease finance. As he qualifies as an SBE, he prepays 12 months of the lease payments, maximising his tax deduction for the 2008 year.

Until they bring in a tax rate of more than 100 per cent, it will always be better to earn extra income. The only time tax may enter into a decision is when the effort required to earn the income is greater than the after-tax benefit you'll receive from it. The bottom line is, income tax should not be avoided at all costs. It should, however, be understood and planned for to make sure you are maximising your income and minimising your tax.

Just the facts, please

Another important thing to understand about income tax is that the facts of each situation are what will determine the outcome. People sometimes try to put different spins on the facts, or even change the facts to suit them, but in the end the ATO will make a decision on the facts alone. And in the end, the burden of proof is on taxpayers, not the tax office.

In very basic terms, there are four ingredients that determine how much tax an individual or business entity pays:

- assessable income
- allowable deductions
- taxable income
- the applicable tax rate.

By subtracting all of your allowable deductions from your total assessable income, your arrive at your taxable income. This figure is then multiplied by the applicable tax rate to calculate the tax you must pay.

Let's look at each of these four ingredients in more detail.

Assessable income

What counts as assessable income? The first factor to consider is whether the income relates to a hobby, or to running a business. If it can be classed as a hobby or a private pastime, the money you receive will not be regarded as income.

How do you know whether you are running a business or engaging in a hobby? If the activity that generates the income is done on a part-time basis and is not organised, you keep no records, take no action to maximise the amounts you receive (by advertising, say), and the prime motivator is enjoyment and not making a profit, the activity will more than likely be a hobby. If not, you are probably running a business.

If you are running a business, you must then work out whether what you are receiving is income, and therefore assessable, or not income, and therefore not assessable. Before giving the plain English explanation, let me give you a peek into the complicated—some would say deranged—minds of the tax legislators. What follows are sections of the legislation, word for word, relating to income:

6-1(1) Assessable income consists of ordinary income and statutory income.

6-1(2) Some ordinary income, and some statutory income, is exempt income.

6-1(3) Exempt income is not assessable income.

6-1(4) Some ordinary income, and some statutory income, is neither assessable income nor exempt income.

6-1(5) An amount of ordinary income or statutory income can have only one status (that is, assessable income, exempt income or non-assessable non-exempt income) in the hands of a particular entity.

Clear as mud really.

Let's try to make this a bit clearer. 'Ordinary income' is something you receive regularly, such as sales, rent, interest and service fees. Money received in one-off amounts, such as the proceeds of a Tattslotto win or the sale of investments, tends to be classed as a windfall gain or capital receipts.

It is appropriate that at this point to explain this concept of a windfall not being assessable income. Unlike the USA, Australia does not tax gambling or prize winnings. This means if you're a weekend punter, the money you win at the races is not assessable. If you receive a gift of cash or an investment from someone, that also is not taxable. However, the person making the gift could be required to pay capital gains tax, if the gift is an asset that has increased in value since he or she bought it.

Income can be received in the form of cash, but it can also be received in other ways. The most common other form is a commitment to be paid in the future—such as when goods and services are sold on credit. No cash is received, but the right to receive cash in the future is granted.

Income can also be received in the form of goods or services, aka bartering. The value of the good or service received is still classed as assessable income. (A section later in this chapter will deal more thoroughly with the tax treatment of bartering.)

'Statutory income' is those amounts that the government, in its wisdom, has decided you must include in your taxable income—usually in order to make the tax treatment of that type of income more certain. The best example of statutory income is the capital gain you make on the sale of an investment.

On the flip side of statutory income is 'exempt income'. This is income that the government has legislated as not being taxable: the most recent example is pension and lump sum payments from a superannuation fund to someone 60 or over. Another good example is the capital gain exempted under the 50 per cent small business active asset exemption. If the relevant tests are passed, this makes 50 per cent of the assessable gain on the sale of a business exempt.

At the risk of confusing you slightly, a new category of income was introduced in 2003–04. It created the possibility of income not being assessable but also not being exempt. Basically, no tax is payable on this income, but it does not fit into any of the other classifications.

The fifth and final clause of that bewildering legal definition is there to protect taxpayers. It means that although an item can be classified as both assessable and statutory income, it can only be taxed once and does not have to be included in two different sections of a tax return or in two different years.

The main point to remember for most people in business is that assessable income is what you receive for the goods or services you sell or provide. When you start getting into the more complicated kinds of potential income, it pays to get good advice from a professional.

Allowable deductions

When you run a business, there are two legal categories — or to use the technical term, 'limbs' — of items that are tax-deductible. They are:

1 those items that are losses or outgoings incurred in producing or gaining assessable income
2 those items that are losses or outgoings necessarily incurred in carrying on a business for the purpose of gaining or producing assessable income.

The first category has broader application than the second, because of the words 'necessarily incurred' in the definition. This qualifier also means, however, that if an expense was incurred that did not have to be, it is not deductible. An example of this would be a manufacturer of knives who decided to undertake a course in physics. The course in physics was done because the topic interested the business owner, not because it was necessary knowledge for making knives, so it would not be an allowable deduction.

The important thing to stress is that there must be a connection between the amount spent and the business income earned for it to be tax-deductible. Even where there is a connection, though, three types of expenditure are not deductible:

- items of a capital, private or domestic nature
- items incurred in gaining or producing exempt income
- items for which the income tax act prevents a tax deduction (for example, the cost of entertaining, fines and bribes).

The second qualifier, items relating to exempt income, is not a common one for small business owners, as they mainly only earn assessable income. The first group of items is the one most frequently encountered. Basically, for an item to be tax-deductible it must relate directly to the production of income.

A purchase that merely enables income to be produced is regarded as a capital cost, and is therefore not wholly deductible in the year it is purchased. A good way to decide whether something is capital in nature is to consider how long it will last. If you buy something that will last for more than 12 months, there's a good chance it is a capital expense.

For example, the cost of buying a factory, shop or office for a business is not deductible. Plant and equipment, vehicles and the goodwill of a business are other examples. Amounts spent maintaining or repairing these capital items, on the other hand, are deductible.

Items that are private or domestic in nature are also not deductible. Some items are clearly private, such as the cost of the electricity you use at home. Others can be used for both business and private purposes, in which case they are either totally non-tax-deductible or only the business component is tax-deductible. Take clothes as an example: unless you live in a nudist colony or like being arrested for indecent exposure, you must wear them. Therefore, where clothes can be worn in both a business and a private or domestic situation, they are not deductible. However, a work uniform that meets all of the requirements is deductible.

Tricky deductions

There are a number of common business expenses that cause problems, due to them sometimes not being tax-deductible or having special rules relating to how the deduction can be claimed. These include:

- bad debts written off
- borrowing costs
- entertainment
- fines
- insurances
- interest paid
- legal fees
- motor vehicle expenses

- power, light and heating
- repairs and maintenance
- replacement of tools
- telephone
- travelling expenses.

We'll look at each of these in turn.

Bad debts written off

Bad debts must be recognised as non-collectable and written off before 30 June each year. Appropriate documentation to support the write-off must be kept—this could include letters from debt collectors or other correspondence that shows the debt cannot be collected.

Borrowing costs

Borrowing costs can be claimed as a deduction over the period of the loan or five years, whichever is the lesser. This means if the loan is for 12 months, the borrowing costs can be written off in the year they are paid. If the loan is for 10 years, the borrowing costs can be written off over five years.

Entertainment

The cost of entertaining, which includes meals, liquor and entertainment, is normally a non-tax-deductible expense. It's only deductible if the entertainment relates to employees and fringe benefits tax has been paid.

Fines

Although a fine can be directly related to earning income—a parking fine when visiting clients, for example—no tax deduction is allowed.

Insurances

Not all insurances are tax-deductible. Fire, theft and accident insurances are deductible when they relate to business items. Life insurance and home insurance, even if you have a home office, are not tax-deductible.

Interest paid

To be deductible, interest must relate to a loan taken out for income-producing or business-related purposes. For more on this, see the 'First principle of borrowing' on page 67.

Legal fees

For legal fees to be tax-deductible, they must relate to an income-earning activity. Thus, legal fees relating to the purchase of a property are not tax-deductible: they are classed as part of the purchase cost. Legal fees relating to collecting outstanding debts, on the other hand, are tax-deductible.

Motor vehicle expenses

You can only claim the costs relating to a car's business usage. The prescribed methods of claiming these deductions is outlined in chapter 11, 'Cars and tax'.

Power, light and heating

If you work from home, you can claim power, light and heating as deductions — just make sure you have a reasonable basis for the amount of business use you claim.

Repairs and maintenance

Repairs are only deductible where the work is done to reinstate equipment and other assets to their original condition. Where the work improves the equipment or asset, it is regarded as a capital cost and if this cost is over \$91 excluding GST it must be depreciated.

Replacement of tools
Tools that have a life of less than 12 months or cost less than \$91 excluding GST can be claimed in full; otherwise they should be depreciated.

Telephone
Where a telephone is used for both business and private purposes, records need to be kept to justify the percentage of business use you claim.

Travelling expenses
Travelling expenses should be divided into local and overseas categories, and only travel that is income-related can be claimed. Travel that relates to capital expenditure, such as travelling to buy an investment property, cannot be claimed. Where overseas or local travel is for an extended period, a travel diary must be kept to justify the business purpose of the trip. The travel diary should also differentiate between business and private travel and ensure only business-related travel costs are claimed.

The burden of proof

It is important to point out that, when it comes to whether an item is business related or not, the burden of proof is on the taxpayer. Often, costs that a business incurs are not claimable in the year they are paid, or are not claimable at all — like fines. For this reason, the accounting profit and the taxable income or profit of a business can be different.

Taxable income and financial statements

Taxable income is calculated by subtracting the total allowable deductions from the total assessable income for the business. In the past, this was often done for a small business by its accountant, but since the introduction of the GST many owners are recording the financial transactions of their business themselves. And as a result, many business owners now have accounting software packages that they use to complete business activity statements. These programs track debtors and accounts payable, and also produce reports showing how much taxable income the business has made for a given period of time.

The problem is, despite business owners receiving these financial statements on a regular basis (whether generated themselves or provided by their accountant), they often don't really understand them or use them to try and improve the business.

The scoreboards in one-day cricket matches are similar to the statements an owner gets. The runs made are, in effect, the income; while the wickets lost are the expenses. Could you imagine playing one-day cricket, or even watching it, if you didn't understand the scoreboard? The same applies to business. To maximise the chance of succeeding in business, you should have a basic understanding of what the financial statements mean.

The basic financial reports for a business fit into two categories. The first category has two statements that show how a business has performed historically: the trading statement and the profit and loss statement. The second category has a statement that provides a snapshot of what the business looks like financially at a given point in time:

the balance sheet. This shows what the company owns, what it owes and how much the owners have invested in the business.

The trading statement

A trading statement shows the total income from the main activities of a business, and those costs that are directly incurred to earn that income. Only costs that have a direct relationship to the income should be included — for example, if a business sells ice-creams, the costs in the trading statement would include ice-cream, cones and extras such as crushed nuts.

The difference between the income and the cost of producing that income is the gross profit of the business. Divide the gross profit by the total income, and you have the gross profit margin. Monitoring your gross profit regularly and comparing it with the average gross profit margins for your industry means you'll detect any operating problems and can take corrective action quickly.

The profit and loss statement

The profit and loss statement shows the fixed or overhead expenses for the business, such as rent, telephone, rates, insurance and salaries — costs that must be paid even if no income is generated. Deduct the total for these from the gross profit and other non-operating income, such as interest, and you have the net profit or loss of the business.

The costs in both the trading statement and the profit and loss statement must only relate to the period being reported on. So, for example, the trading stock at the end of a period must be deducted from the purchase costs of the goods, so that only the costs of the goods sold during that period are shown on the trading statement. This cost of stock is shown as an asset in the balance sheet instead, and carried forward as a cost for the next period.

A number of other costs also benefit future periods and should not be included. For example, the cost of an ice-cream machine that will last five years is not shown on the profit and loss statement, but is shown in the balance sheet. In this case, the cost is divided by how long the machine is expected to last, and that amount is claimed each year as depreciation.

When the gross profit margin is known, you can use the business's fixed costs to calculate how much income you need to generate to break even. For example, a lawnmower shop that has overheads of $50 000 a year and a gross profit margin of 50 per cent must produce $100 000 in income to break even.

The balance sheet

If the profit and loss statement is the scoreboard, the balance sheet is like an X-ray. It provides a picture of what a business is made up of at a particular point in time, and when analysed properly can be used to predict future financial problems. It is often used by third parties such as banks to provide information on the viability of a business.

In its most simple form, a balance sheet should be a summary of how much a business is worth. It shows what assets a business has, how much it owes and what its value is to the owners. And nearly every item on it should be capable of being verified or reconciled. For example, an amount shown as owing on a bank loan should agree with a loan statement; the value listed for trading stock on hand should agree with a stocktake.

Where items on a balance sheet are wrong, the result shown on the profit and loss statement will also be wrong. This is because all the items on a balance sheet have a direct effect on the profit and loss of a business — if the amount shown for a bank loan is understated, say, the profit will be overstated because interest has not been accounted for. Conversely, if the loan is overstated the profit will be understated, because principal repayments may have been shown as an expense.

A common mistake made by business owners who prepare their own financial statements is not to reconcile three of the main items on a balance sheet regularly: the bank, debtors and creditors. If you don't do this at least monthly, the job of detecting errors is made that much harder — and more costly if your accountant has to find the errors.

The equity section

The main components of a balance sheet are equity, assets and liabilities. The equity section shows how much capital has been invested by the owners and how much profit has been made and accumulated after taxes. Clearly, a business with not much capital, and either accumulated losses or very little in accumulated profits, is not in a strong financial position!

The asset section

The asset section of a balance sheet is split into four sub-categories. The first is current assets: assets such as stock and debtors that should be turned into cash within 12 months. By carefully reviewing what's included in current assets, the efficiency of a business can often be improved. A business that regularly reviews its debtors for bad debts and has a tight credit policy, for example, will have a better cash flow than one that does not.

The next subcategory is non-current assets, which consists of assets that will not be turned into cash within 12 months — perhaps a mortgage investment that will mature in three years, or a term deposit. The third subcategory is fixed assets. This covers items that are not easily converted into cash, and includes things such as land, buildings, plant and equipment. Fixed assets should be regularly reviewed for items that have no value, and these should be written off.

The last subcategory is intangible assets: items that are not physical assets but still have a value, such as goodwill or the cost of taking out a patent. Goodwill is often only shown if the business was purchased and goodwill was included in the purchase price. It should reflect what the business is worth, and is usually directly related to profitability.

The liabilities section

The liabilities section of the balance sheet is divided into two categories: current liabilities and non-current liabilities. Current liabilities are debts that must be paid within 12 months, and can include accounts payable and amounts owed to the tax office for income tax, PAYG withholding and GST. Non-current liabilities are those debts that a business will not have to pay in under 12 months, such as long-term bank loans or hire-purchase contracts.

The working capital ratio

The working capital ratio is an important indicator of the financial health of a business, as it tells you how easily the business can meet its liabilities. It's arrived at by dividing total current assets by total current liabilities. A ratio of less than one is usually an indicator of a business in financial distress, as it means the business has more current liabilities than current assets; a ratio of between one and two indicates that the business is in a strong position and should be able to withstand short-term business problems. A ratio of more than two could mean that the business is carrying excess stock, or is not managing its cash and accounts receivable resources efficiently.

Tax rates

Once a business has worked out its taxable income figure, by subtracting its total allowable deductions from its total assessable income, how much tax it then pays depends on the type of business structure used.

Where a company has been used, or a company is a partner, unitholder or beneficiary of a trust, tax will be paid at the company tax rate. In nearly all other cases, tax will be paid at the individual's applicable marginal tax rate (see table 1 in the appendix). The only time that a different tax rate would be paid is in the case of a discretionary trust that has not distributed all of its taxable income to beneficiaries. This does not happen very often, however, as the trustee pays tax on income that is not distributed, at the top marginal tax rate for individuals.

Depending on a person's age and level of taxable income, the tax payable amount can then be reduced by tax offsets.

Some of the more common that can apply to business owners are the low-income offset, the dependant offset and the entrepreneurs' offset (see the appendix for the full list).

In addition to paying income tax, of course, individuals also pay the Medicare levy when their taxable income exceeds the relevant threshold (the threshold differs depending on whether you are single or married, and the number of children you have). When your income is in between the shading-in thresholds, the formula for calculating the Medicare levy is so complicated it would give Albert Einstein a headache.

When a person has income over a certain amount and does not have private health insurance, yet another tax is payable—the Medicare levy surcharge. For individuals with income of more than $49 999 and couples with income of more than $99 999, the surcharge is 1 per cent. It does not make sense to pay the surcharge—taking out private health insurance will not cost you much more, and at least then you are getting a benefit for the money you're paying out. (Note: if the change announced if the 2008 Budget is passed the surcharge will not be paid until an individual's income exceeds $99 999 or a couple's exceeds $149 999.)

Let's look now at an example of how income tax is calculated. Fred runs a dance studio; his wife Ginger does not work, and spends her time making ballroom dresses. For the 2008 year the business has the results shown in table 4.1.

Table 4.1: Fred's business

	$
Total assessable income	70 000
Less total deductible expenses	40 000
Total taxable income	**30 000**

Fred qualifies for the low-income and dependent spouse offsets, so the tax he pays is calculated as shown in table 4.2.

Table 4.2: Fred's tax

	$	$
Taxable income		30 000
Tax payable at 15 per cent after tax-free threshold		3600
Less		
Low-income offset	750	
Dependent spouse offset	2100	
Total offsets		**2850**
Net tax payable		750
Medicare levy		175
Total tax payable		**925**

This brings us back to my original point about income tax: if you have organised yourself correctly to ensure you are paying the lowest amount of tax you legally can, I hope you are paying a lot of it! Because if you are, you are running a successful business and making lots of money.

The tax principles of business borrowing

As a chartered accountant, I'm asked many tax and business questions by clients. By far the most common question relates to the borrowing of money for business or private reasons, and its effect on income tax. Despite all the different sorts of finance available and the different reasons people have for borrowing, there are five basic principles that everyone can follow.

First principle of borrowing

The first principle of borrowing can best be described as the golden rule of borrowing. Put simply: 'Where possible, borrow for business and pay cash for private'. When you borrow for private items, such as the family home or a holiday, none of the interest is tax-deductible, and if you are paying the top tax rate this means you will have to earn almost twice as much to pay the interest charged. For example, $1000 of income would be needed to repay $1000 of tax-deductible interest, but if that interest is not tax-deductible, on the top tax rate you'll need $1869 of income to repay it.

Second principle of borrowing

The second principle of borrowing is an extension of the golden rule: 'Borrow principal and interest for private purposes, and interest only for business purposes'. When this rule is followed, your tax-efficient borrowings remain the same while you're paying off the non-tax-deductible borrowing. Once the private loan is repaid, you can then start to repay the business loan.

At this point it is important to understand how the tax law works in relation to deductions for interest paid. There is a common misconception that where an income-producing property is used as security for a loan, the interest will be tax-deductible. Nothing could be further from the truth.

Under Australian tax law, it is *why* the loan was taken out and how the money is spent that dictates whether a tax deduction can be claimed. So, for example, say that a husband and wife have a principal residence, no loans outstanding, and want to upgrade to a new home but keep the old one as an investment property. No tax deduction would be allowed for the interest on the new loan, because even though they borrowed so that they could rent out the existing property, the proceeds of the loan were used to buy a private residence.

If, on the other hand, the couple sells their existing home and uses the sale proceeds to buy a new home, once they settle into the new home they can borrow against it to buy an investment property. In this case, even though the private home is used as security, the interest is tax-deductible because the loan proceeds are used to purchase the investment property.

Third principle of borrowing

The third principle of borrowing is: 'Where possible, keep business and private loans separate.' If a loan is made up of both business and private borrowings, the loan repayments decrease both the private and business loans in proportion—which goes against the second principle of borrowing.

To continue the previous example, if the couple buying the new home had to borrow $30000 for the home and $120000 for the rental property, they should take out a principal and interest loan of $30000 and an interest-only loan of $120000. This would mean all principal repayments go to decreasing the private loan, while the tax-deductible loan stays the same.

Fourth principle of borrowing

The fourth principle of borrowing is: 'Fit the finance to the purpose of the loan'. There are four main types of finance available. The first type requires security in the form of land or buildings, and you are only able to borrow up to the maximum percentage of the value of the security that the lender allows. Mortgage loans offered by banks and other lending institutions are of this type. Traditionally, they have lower interest rates than the alternatives, are for larger amounts and are paid off over a longer period. They should be used to fund large purchases such as properties and businesses.

The second type of finance uses 100 per cent of the asset being purchased as security, and includes leases, chattel mortgages and hire-purchase. They have a higher interest rate than mortgages, are repaid over a shorter period, and often require the borrower to pay a lump sum amount at the end. Leases and hire-purchase are used to best effect when you do not want to tie up a main asset as security and cannot be bothered doing the paperwork for a mortgage loan.

The term of this type of finance should be dictated by how long the asset being purchased will last. If you were buying a motor vehicle or piece of machinery, say, a five-year term would be appropriate; if you were purchasing a computer that may become obsolete in a relatively short time, a three-year term would be more applicable.

The third type of finance uses non-tangible business assets such as accounts receivable or goodwill as security, and usually has the highest rate of interest. This type of borrowing is quite often regarded as a last resort to keep a business going: this may have been true in the past, but it is now becoming more user-friendly and less costly.

The fourth type of finance tends to require the same type of security as a bank loan, but the finance fluctuates in value depending on business requirements—bank overdrafts and home equity loans are two examples. Due to the higher interest rate on overdrafts they should only be used to fund temporary business shortfalls, not for long-term borrowing.

Fifth principle of borrowing

The final principle of borrowing is: 'Before entering into a finance contract, look around at the alternatives and then seek advice from your accountant'. It might take extra time to do this and cost a few extra dollars in accounting fees, but you could save a lot of money by getting the right sort of finance in the most tax-effective way.

The trap of the black economy

Contrary to popular belief, the introduction of the GST and the Australian business number (ABN) system in July 2000 was never meant to wipe out the black economy. The blackmarket will not die as long as there are banknotes in circulation; at best, the new tax system was only ever hoped to reduce some of the tax being lost.

However, the introduction of the ABN system, under which a tax liability is placed on the payer as well as the person receiving the money, has meant more income is now being returned as assessable income from some sources. One example is the entertainment industry: prior to the introduction of the ABN regulations, a lot of bands were paid in cash, but afterward many bands had to register for an ABN to avoid losing 48.5 per cent in ABN withholding tax.

I personally have not seen any proof that the black economy has grown since the introduction of the GST. What is certain is that, since its introduction, 10 per cent in GST has been paid in almost every situation where cash is spent.

Many businesses don't think through the ramifications of skimming off a large percentage of their cash income. Sometimes, the amounts of cash being diverted are so large that the tax office finds it relatively easy to detect tax avoidance. Detection has also been made easier by the industry-specific statistics the tax office is amassing—the ATO can check a business's figures against industry ratios and identify tax avoidance by extremely low profit margins or unusually high expense ratios. Also, once it suspects that tax avoidance is taking place it is much easier to estimate how much has been avoided. I recently heard of one campaign by the tax office, for example, that concentrated on strawberry-growers. The tax office multiplied the number of punnets purchased by an estimated selling value for each punnet, and then estimated how much income each grower should have declared. The actual income they declared was deducted from this estimate to arrive at the amount of income not declared.

Another way the tax office can estimate how much income has not been declared is when cash is used to buy the necessities of life. Too often, people spend black money on groceries, mortgage repayments and other household costs. Where taxpayers cannot demonstrate that they funded these purchases through, say, a salary from the business, the tax evasion is fairly obvious.

On the other hand, when black money is spent on non-essential items like restaurant meals, alcohol, holidays and entertainment, the tax office finds it harder to detect. The problem is, of course, many people find they have little to show for years of tax evasion except for an expanded waistline or a drinking problem. If they'd declared the income instead and put it into superannuation, they would have paid tax on the income at the lowest rate and increased their net worth.

Business problems may also be caused when large amounts of cash are not put through the business. For starters, it reduces the profitability of the business, so if the business needs to borrow money for expansion or a major asset purchase, it will not be able to demonstrate to financiers that it can afford the loan repayments.

Another problem arises when the owner wants to sell the business. A common determinant of the goodwill value of a business is its sustainable net profit: when profitability has been continuously reduced by stripping cash out, it's a lot harder to get a good price for the business. A nudge and a wink to a prospective buyer when telling them how much cash you have been taking over the years is a poor substitute for tax return figures that accurately show how much profit has been made year after year.

CHAPTER 5

Paying your employees and your income tax as you go

When you run a business and want it to grow, there are two inevitabilities. The first is the need to take on employees, because you can't do everything yourself. The second is the amount of tax you are paying can increase to the point that you are caught up in the Pay As You Go (PAYG) instalments system. This chapter takes you through the things you need to know when you employ people—even yourself—and how PAYG instalments work.

The PAYG withholding system

When a business employs people—even when the business owner employs himself or herself through a trust or company structure—it must deduct tax from most of the payments it makes to those employees. So, for example, if a sole trader decided to start operating the business through a company structure and pay himself or herself a wage, that money would be subject to PAYG withholding.

What payments are taxed?

PAYG withholding must be deducted, not only from the gross amount of salary or wages, but also from:

- director's fees

- allowances for employees, such as car and tools
- payments to contractors who have a voluntary agreement
- eligible termination payments
- payments to suppliers who do not quote an ABN
- return to work incentives.

There are two payments to employees that do not require PAYG withholding amounts to be deducted—living-away-from-home allowances, and reimbursements for expenses the employee has paid on behalf of the business. This includes things like parking expenses and meal costs while travelling on business. However, if it is a payment for car expenses using the kilometre method, PAYG withholding must be deducted.

How do you know how much tax you take out?

The amount of tax deducted from payments to employees depends on whether the employee has provided a tax file number (TFN) on a declaration form. If the TFN has not been quoted, tax must be deducted at the top marginal rate plus Medicare levy—46.5 per cent. Where a TFN declaration has been quoted, tax is deducted in accordance with a schedule issued by the ATO.

In some cases, these schedules are mailed out automatically by the ATO; otherwise, they are available from the ATO and from some post offices. If you have a computer payroll package, it will have the tax rates loaded as part of the system.

The payment process

The process of paying wages is shown in table 5.1.

Table 5.1: the process of paying wages

Step 1	Work out how much an employee has earned in salary or wages for the period.
Step 2	Add to this amount any allowances payable.
Step 3	Calculate the tax payable on this total, using the appropriate schedule.
Step 4	Deduct this tax amount from the total worked out at step 2.
Step 5	Pay the employee the net amount after tax.
Step 6	Keep a record of the total amounts of PAYG withholding deducted for the period.

Employers must pay PAYG withholding to the tax office by certain deadlines, depending on their classification:

- 'Large employers' are those that deduct more than $1 million in PAYG withholding from employees a year. They must pass on the tax they deduct to the ATO electronically within approximately a week of making the deduction.

- 'Medium employers' are those that deduct between $25 001 and $1 million in PAYG withholding a year. They must pass on the tax deducted to the ATO by the 21st day of the month following the month it was deducted. If they lodge a BAS return quarterly, they can pay each third month's tax by the 28th of the month following the end of the quarter, except for December, when they must pay by February 28.

- 'Small employers' are those that deduct up to $25 000 in PAYG withholding a year. If the employer is not registered for GST, it must pay the ATO quarterly by the 21st day of the month following the end of the quarter. If it is registered for GST, the PAYG withholding must be paid by the 28th day of the month following each quarter, except for the December quarter, when it must be paid by February 28.

The low threshold for PAYG withholding payments means that small businesses with as few as five employees may be required to lodge two monthly BAS returns a quarter. In addition, a quarterly BAS will need to be lodged, giving a mixture of monthly figures for PAYG withholding tax and quarterly figures for GST and PAYG instalments of income tax.

The trap for personal services income businesses

Where a business caught by the personal services income (PSI) laws makes a quarterly profit (after allowing for salaries paid and the limited deductions allowable), PAYG withholding must be paid on this profit as if the individual providing the service had earned it. This profit is called 'attributable income' and effectively means that a PSI business cannot make a profit.

The PAYG withholding tax on the attributable income must be paid to the tax office by the 28th day of the month following the quarter when the income was earned. This means that PSI businesses must complete full quarterly financial accounts to meet all of their commitments under the PSI laws.

The superannuation guarantee system

The superannuation guarantee system (SGS) requires employers to make super contributions on behalf of employees, calculated as a percentage of the employee's salaries and wages. For the 2008–09 year, the compulsory SGS contribution was 9 per cent.

Employers do receive a tax deduction for these contributions. However, the SGS is the harshest, most complex and most inflexible system administered by the ATO. For starters, if an employer meets all the requirements, it gets a tax deduction for the SGS contribution; but if it is even one day late, it must pay the contribution plus penalties — which are not tax-deductible.

Who's considered an 'employee'?

The complexity of the SGS begins with the definition of who is an employee for SGS purposes: as well as traditional employees, the term can cover contractors that do not work through a company structure. The questions you need to answer when deciding whether a contractor counts as an 'employee' include:

- Is the contractor directed on how to perform the work rather than them deciding independently?
- Could the work be done by someone else, instead of the contractor? In other words, can the contractor have someone else do the work, or must he or she do it?
- Are you, rather than the contractor, supplying the tools or equipment required to do the job?
- Does the contractor gets paid for the hours worked, not for producing a result?

- Is the contractor told the hours he or she must work, instead of deciding independently?

If the answer to all these question is yes, it's likely that the contractor will be classed an employee—however, the facts of each case will decide for certain.

What salary and wages do you use to calculate SG contributions?

The next complication of the SGS is the types of salary and wages used for calculating the 9 per cent compulsory super contribution. In some cases, the salary or wages to be included are defined by a super fund, a law of the Commonwealth, a state or a territory, an industrial award or an agreement with employees. However, where none of these apply, a default earnings base called 'ordinary times earnings' must be used. Only an employee's earnings for the ordinary hours worked are included in ordinary times earnings: overtime is excluded.

Here's a fairly comprehensive list of what's generally counted as salary and wages for super contributions:

- allowances for such things as travel, tools or work sites
- bonuses relating to normal hours worked
- commissions
- over-award payments
- shift loading
- casual loadings
- workers compensation payments
- pay for annual leave, long service leave and sick leave taken
- director's fees.

Payments to employees that are not counted as salary and wages are:

- reimbursed expenses
- overtime
- Christmas bonuses
- benefits subject to FBT
- payments for maternity or paternity leave
- annual leave loading
- payments for annual leave, long service leave and sick leave paid as a lump sum when an employee is terminated
- payments in lieu of notice
- redundancy payments.

In addition, a maximum level is placed on the earnings of an employee for super guarantee purposes. The maximum salary or wage for the 2006–07 year was $35 240 a quarter. So, once an employee's salary or wages exceed this limit, the employer is not obligated to make super contributions on the excess.

Deadlines for SG contributions

The SG contribution must be paid quarterly by employers by no later than the 28th of the month following the end of the quarter the contributions relate to. This means the deadlines are April 28 for the March quarter, the July 28 for the June quarter, the October 28 for the September quarter, and January 28 for the December quarter.

When an employer either pays a contribution late, or does not pay the correct amount, it is required to pay a super guarantee charge. In this situation, it must send a superannuation guarantee statement to the tax office by the 28th day of the second month following the end of the quarter.

For a more complete explanation of the SGS and its implications for employers, please refer to the relevant chapter in my book *Super Made Simple: A Survival Guide*, published by John Fairfax Publications Pty Ltd.

Workers' insurance

When you start a business, there are many things to consider and arrange. What sort of business structure should you use? How much working capital will you need? What insurance policies should you take out? If your business is going to employ people, even yourself, you must take out WorkCover insurance. The problem is, the legislation that regulates WorkCover is harsh and unforgiving—business owners face huge penalties if they make even an innocent mistake.

There are several situations in which business owners could find themselves in trouble and subject to heavy penalties, including:

- if they do not register for WorkCover in time.
  Employers must register for WorkCover within 14 days of starting to employ people; if they don't register within the time limit, a penalty of 100 per cent of the premium that was paid late can be imposed. It is therefore extremely important that when you start a business you register for WorkCover at the same time as you register with the tax office as an employer.

- if they underestimate the total amount they will pay for wages in a year.

- if they are incorrectly classified for WorkCover purposes, and pay too much, or too little WorkCover insurance.

- if they do not realise they must pay a higher or lower WorkCover premium due to grouping provisions. In some states, grouping provisions combine the salary and wages for several employers and treat them as if they were one employer, and this often results in the predominant activity of the group applying to all or most group members. For example, say a barbecue manufacturer starts up a new business selling gas fittings—this entity could be grouped with the barbecue business and would therefore pay the higher WorkCover premium for manufacturing businesses.

Who do you take WorkCover out through?

Although each state has an authority with ultimate responsibility for regulating workers' insurance, the insurance cover itself is taken out through insurance companies. WorkCover premiums should not differ between the different insurance companies because the WorkCover legislation sets the rates. The rates differ depending on the industry that the employer is in: industries with a history of having a higher number of work accidents, such as the building industry, pay a higher premium.

Unfortunately, the WorkCover legislation has been drawn in such a way that business owners carry all of the responsibility. If an insurance company misclassifies a workplace, it is the responsibility of the business owner to detect the error and have the classification amended. However, in Victoria for example, if an employer discovers that its WorkCover classification is incorrect, any retrospective premium adjustment is confined to the commencement of the current financial year instead of being backdated to when the insurance cover commenced—provided the employer did not mislead the insurer when registering for WorkCover.

Penalties can also be imposed when an employer underestimates the amount of salaries and wages that it will be paying for a year. The insurance premium is based on an estimate of the total payroll figure for the next 12 months, an amount that includes fringe benefits and super. Where an employer underestimates this by more than 20 per cent, it faces penalties of 100 per cent on the underpaid premium.

The inclusion of superannuation as wages for WorkCover purposes hits small business owners unjustly. It's reasonable to include amounts paid to employees under the super-annuation guarantee regime, as this benefit was introduced by a federal Labor government in lieu of pay increases. However, often a business owner will make super contributions well in excess of what he or she has to under the super guarantee system. It makes sense from an economic point of view for business owners to reduce profits this way—not only do they pay less tax, but they also help to ensure that they will not have to rely on government benefits when they retire.

Enforcement and common breaches

To ensure that all employers meet their workers compen-sation responsibilities, two types of enforcement practice are carried out. The first type is the health and safety inspections that are done to ensure safe work practices. The second type is the audits that are carried out by the WorkCover authorities in each state and territory.

WorkCover authorities all have access to a large database, and also exchange information with other state revenue offices. This enables them to have audit systems in place that are extremely thorough. As well as misclassification of an employer's predominant activity, audits often discover breaches such as:

- understating the total amount of remuneration paid to employees. This area is very complex, and employers can inadvertently make mistakes due to not fully understanding what must be included as remuneration—that is, all amounts paid to employees and some contractors.

- not including amounts paid to contractors that are caught for WorkCover purposes. This breach makes up around 48 per cent of all WorkCover errors.

In some states and territories, the WorkCover definitions of 'contractor' are closely aligned with the payroll tax definition. This means if the payment to the contractor is caught by payroll tax, it is automatically caught for WorkCover.

It does not matter, with regard to WorkCover, if the subcontractor you hire operates through a company. There are two provisions within the legislation that deal with contractors: one concentrates on all types of contractors (sole traders, partnerships, trusts, companies) and the other deals only with contractors that are natural persons (although that can still include partnerships and trusts).

The legislation that relates to all types of contractors has a number of exceptions, while the legislation relating to contractors who are natural persons is far stricter, with few exceptions. This approach is in line with the overall concept of WorkCover being there to protect workers: unincorporated contractors do not technically pay themselves wages, and therefore cannot 'cover themselves' for WorkCover, so those who hire them are most at risk. And by the way, you cannot escape your legal liability to take out workers compensation insurance by entering into an agreement with a contractor (or employee) that nullifies the obligation.

What is more alarming is that even if you can hire an incorporated contractor who is registered for WorkCover and pays a premium on its own wages, this does not automatically relieve you of the liability for workers compensation insurance for that contractor. Unless the legislation specifically excludes the payment to the incorporated contractor, you must include it as part of your WorkCover remuneration. This can often lead to a double payment of WorkCover premium.

The WorkCover systems in each state and territory are very rigid and very unforgiving. If you are unsure whether you are meeting your obligations, or feel that you have been classified incorrectly and are paying too high a premium, you should speak to your accountant or someone who specialises in WorkCover insurance.

The PAYG instalments system

As I mentioned in chapter 1, the PAYG instalments system was introduced to replace the old provisional tax system, and to put people who earn business or investment income on a more equal footing with people who are employed.

People who earn salary and wages have income tax deducted every pay period by their employer, in the form of

PAYG withholding. This means that their disposable income is reduced when they receive it. People with investments or in business, by contrast, receive all of their income, as no tax is deducted. Without PAYG instalments they would only pay income tax after they lodge their tax return, up to 10 months after the end of the financial year in which the income was earned.

Who is liable to pay PAYG instalments?

To be liable for PAYG instalments, you must receive a notice from the Australian Taxation Office. PAYG instalments are payable when a taxpayer:

- receives more than $2000 in investment or business income, not including capital gains
- receives a tax assessment showing tax payable of more than $500
- has a notional tax amount of more than $250
- is not entitled to a senior Australian tax offset.

The ATO calculates notional tax by increasing your business and investment income shown on your last tax return to reflect what they think the economy will grow by in the next year. Tax is then calculated on this predicted income at your marginal rate—the amount of income at which notional tax exceeds $250 will therefore differ between taxpayers. For example, the $250 threshold will not be exceeded for someone paying tax at the lowest tax rate (15 per cent) until he or she earns more than $1666, while at the top tax rate of 45 per cent, income of just $556 will mean the threshold is exceeded.

Payments and deadlines

For most taxpayers, PAYG instalments must be paid either annually or quarterly. To be eligible to pay annual instalments you must have less than $8000 in notional tax and not be registered for GST. Annual instalments are payable on the 21 October following the end of the financial year in which the income was earned. If you're not eligible to pay an annual instalment, you will be required to pay quarterly instalments. These are due on the 28th day of the month following the end of each quarter.

Companies, superannuation funds and sole traders pay their PAYG instalments on their business activity statements. Partners in partnerships, beneficiaries of trusts, and individuals who earn investment income or business income and are not registered for GST pay using an instalment activity statement (IAS).

Instalments can be charged in the form of a stated amount or as a percentage of income, and flexibility has been built into the PAYG system to allow taxpayers to vary the instalment amount or instalment rate given by the tax office. For example, where a person's circumstances have changed from one year to the next due to decreased investment earnings or less profitable trading conditions, the PAYG instalment can be varied downward. Care must be taken when varying a PAYG instalment, however, as penalties in the form of interest charges are imposed if less than 85 per cent of the actual tax payable is paid as a result.

When the income tax assessment for the year is issued, the PAYG instalments paid are deducted from the actual tax payable. For example, if PAYG instalments of $4000 were paid for the 2008 tax year, and the actual tax payable on net taxable income was $5000, a final amount of $1000 would be payable when the income tax assessment for 2008 is issued.

CHAPTER 6

Capital gains tax

All small businesses are owned by individuals, even when they use a company, so as well as income tax, there is another tax that can adversely affect them if they do not take it into account—capital gains tax.

Prior to the introduction of capital gains tax on 20 September 1985, the burden of proof was on the tax office. For tax to be payable on an asset, it had to be proven that the asset had been purchased with the intention of making a profit. The system revolved entirely around proving why an asset had been purchased, case by case, to decide whether it was taxable or not.

If someone purchased a holiday house in the 1950s and could show that it had been used regularly for holidays, no tax was payable on the profit when the property was sold. The same went for works of art purchased for their artistic merits and hung on walls for the enjoyment of their owners. The law clearly had a big loophole, and people and corporations exploited the system to make huge tax-free profits.

The introduction of CGT

When most tax loopholes are closed, the measures imposed to begin with are often at their harshest, and are modified over time. Capital gains tax is no exception. When it was first introduced the rules were very simple. Any assets purchased pre 20 September 1985 were exempt from capital gains tax. Any assets purchased after that date, and owned for more than 12 months, were liable for capital gains tax.

Strictly speaking, in fact, there's no such thing as capital gains tax. What we have is a system that sets out how a taxable capital gain is calculated; this assessable gain is then included as taxable income and income tax is paid on it.

Originally, tax was payable on the total capital gain of any asset sold. There were very few exceptions other than a person's home and motor vehicles, and there was only one concession that tried to ensure taxpayers did not pay tax at a higher marginal tax rate than normal. This was called the 'averaging method' and was replaced by a new method called the 'indexation method' that discounted the capital gain to reflect the effect of inflation. It meant taxpayers only paid tax on the capital gain after discounting it for inflation during the time the asset was owned. However, the indexation method was only introduced for assets owned by individuals, complying superannuation funds and trusts. People owning assets through companies were effectively disadvantaged, because they paid tax on the total capital gain made.

The next change came when the indexation rate was frozen at the inflation rate applying at 30 September 1999. Instead of applying a discount based on inflation, the discount became a flat 50 per cent—as a result, when an asset had been owned for more than 12 months income tax was paid on only half of the gain made.

As a general rule, investment assets are still best owned by individuals as opposed to companies. A company does not receive the 50 per cent general discount on a capital gain, but instead pays tax on the whole gain.

Purchasing and selling dates

Under income tax law, the relevant date for purchasing or selling an asset is not the date settlement takes place, but the date of the contract. For share transactions this is not a problem, as in normal circumstances it is only a matter of days between a sale or purchase taking place and the funds being transferred. But with property transactions it can become an issue: they usually take between 60 and 90 days, and sometimes can take longer than 120 days, and so can easily straddle two tax years.

Where a sale note to sell a property is signed in one tax year and settlement takes place in the following year, the relevant sale date for capital gains tax purposes is the earlier tax year. To add to the confusion, even if the sale is conditional upon the purchaser getting finance or selling another property, the sale date will still be the date the sale note was signed.

Taxpayers who are selected for an audit and have incorrectly shown a capital gain in a later tax year are issued with an amended income tax assessment for the earlier year. In this situation the ATO does not impose incorrect return penalties, but an interest penalty is charged and offset with interest paid by the ATO on the tax paid on the capital gain incorrectly shown in the later year.

Calculating capital gain on a property

When calculating the capital gain made on the sale of a property, all associated costs can be used to decrease the profit made. These include:

- purchase costs such as stamp duty and legal fees
- the costs associated with maintaining the property
- selling costs like real estate agents' sales commissions.

Where the property was used for rental purposes, most holding costs will have already been claimed against the rental income. Properties that have been used for private purposes, however, such as holiday homes, will have a greater number of holding costs that can be used to decrease the capital gain. These costs include:

- council rates
- interest on any loans taken out to buy the property
- water rates
- repairs and maintenance
- the cost of any improvements or additions made to the property.

Once all costs have been taken into account, tax will be payable on half of the capital gain remaining.

Here's an example of how capital gains tax works. Simon and Anne purchased a holiday house in 1996. The house cost them $120 000, with $4000 of stamp duty and other costs. In 2000 they borrowed $40 000 to do some renovations and extensions. In the 2008 year they sold the house for $410 000. Over the 12 years of owning the house, they paid $10 000 in council rates.

In 2008 Simon's only source of income was his salary of $180 000, while Anne did not work and had no investment income. Capital gains tax will be paid as shown in table 6.1, overleaf.

Table 6.1: Simon and Anne's CGT

	$	$
Selling value of house		410 000
Less		
Agents' selling commission	12 000	
Adjustment for rates, etc	1 000	
		13 000
Net sale proceeds received		**397 000**
Less purchase and holding costs		
Original cost	120 000	
Stamp duty, etc.	4 000	
Extension	40 000	
Interest on loan for extension	23 000	
Council rates	10 000	
		197 000
Capital gain		200 000
Less 50 per cent general discount		100 000
Taxable gain		**100 000**

Due to Simon's salary, he will pay tax at the top tax rate on his $50 000 share of the gain. This means he pays $23 250. Anne will pay income tax on her share of the gain of $10 350.

Capital gains and your home

Nearly everyone will at some time pay capital gains tax. It could be as the result of selling a business; it could also happen as the result of an inheritance. Before the small business CGT concessions were introduced (we'll look at these in detail in chapter 12), the only major asset that received special treatment was a person's home.

As usual, this tax exemption comes with limitations and conditions. The major ones are that the property must have been a home for the whole time it was owned, must not have been used to produce assessable income, and had a maximum land area of two hectares. This last condition means that where a home is on more than two hectares, the gain made on the extra land will incur capital gains tax when sold. A house on less than two hectares can also incur capital gains tax if the original block purchased is subdivided—where the original home is retained and the vacant block sold, capital gains tax will, in most cases, be payable. However, if a new home is built and on the vacant block instead, and the original home sold, there should be no capital gains tax liability.

The requirements that the house must have been lived in all the time and must not have produced any income have one big exception. Where a person has to move for work or other reasons, the family home can be rented and the exemption retained. To remain eligible for the exemption, the person cannot be absent for more than six years continuously and cannot nominate another house as the principle residence. The absence can be longer than six years altogether, however, as long as he or she returns to live in the house before the first six-year period has expired.

Also, when a person purchases another home and rents his or her old home, the CGT exemption is not totally lost. In this situation, any capital gain made when the original house is sold is apportioned between the periods of ownership, and the capital gain relating to the time the house was used as a principal residence is exempt. Say that a couple bought a home in 1992 for $120 000, lived there until 1997, then bought another home and rented the first one. If the first house was sold in 2002 for $220 000, half of the gain of $100 000 would be exempt.

CGT and home offices

Small business owners can find they have an unexpected capital gains tax bill if they use part of their home for business purposes. For a house to qualify as a place of business, various conditions must be met, such as a separate entrance. Meeting these conditions means that a portion of the rates and interest costs for the home can be claimed as a tax deduction; but the portion of the house used for business purposes also becomes liable for capital gains tax.

Where a home was used as a place of business after 20 August 1996, special rules apply for calculating what is taxable. Effectively, the ownership of the home is split into two—the period when it was used purely as a home (if any) and the period when there was business use. For the period when the home was just a residence, no capital gain tax will be payable on any increase in the value. If a home is used for business purposes from the date it is purchased, however, it will always have a business-period-use component.

For the business period, capital gains tax will be payable on the business proportion of the increase in the value for that time. This is calculated by deducting the value of the home, at the time its use changed or was purchased, from the selling value, and then multiplying the resulting figure by the percentage that the business portion of the home is of the total area. To ensure capital gains tax is minimised, a written valuation should be obtained when the business use commences.

Let's look at an example of how this works. Say an architect decides to start a business, and an office is built as an extension to his home. The house was purchased in 1988 at a cost of $150 000; at the time the office extension was completed and the business use commenced, in 1998, it was worth $220 000. The office makes up 10 per cent of the total area of the house. The house is sold in 2008 for $400 000, and the gain of $70 000 from 1988 to 1998 is tax free. Ten per cent of the $180 000 gain during the time the house was used for business purposes will be counted for capital gains tax.

The taxing matter of death

When a person dies, the tax payable on their assets differs depending on what the asset is and when it was purchased. Certain assets, such as a person's home and superannuation, receive special tax treatment.

The proceeds of a deceased's superannuation, when paid to his or her dependants, are not taxable. For superannuation purposes, a 'dependant' includes a person's spouse, children and any other people that they are interdependent with. In most cases, children are under 18 will be classed as dependants. 'Interdependency' is defined as a relationship between two people, where they have a close personal relationship, they live together, one or both provide financial support for each other, and one or both provide domestic support and personal care. The interdependency test is not so strict that all of the conditions must be met, however; instead, it provides a broad framework, and the facts of each case are taken into account to determine whether a person is a dependant or not.

The tax treatment of assets other than superannuation depends on when they were purchased. Apart from the family home and superannuation, all assets, whether inherited directly or sold by the executor of the estate, will incur capital gains tax.

If the executor of the estate is selling the assets, the date the deceased purchased the asset is used to decide how much CGT is payable. Any assets purchased before September 1985 will be tax-free. However, if the asset was owned by the deceased for more than 12 months, tax is paid on half of the gain; if the asset was owned for less than 12 months, tax is payable on the full gain. Where the will allows it, and the beneficiary is happy to receive the asset instead of the proceeds from sale, a better tax result can be achieved by transferring the ownership of it to the beneficiary instead.

The capital gains tax treatment of the asset in such cases, again, differs depending on when they were purchased. Assets purchased by the deceased before September 1985 are taken to have been purchased by the beneficiary at market value on the date of the deceased's death. Where the assets were purchased by the deceased after September 1985, their purchase price is the purchase price paid by the deceased. For example, say that in 2003 Mary inherits 1000 BHP shares and 1000 NAB shares from her father. The BHP shares were purchased in 1979 for $2000, and the NAB shares in 1990 for $6000. In 2003, the BHP shares were worth $6000.

In July 2006 Mary needs a new car, so she sells all of the shares: she gets $26 000 for the BHP ones and $34 000 for the NAB. As the BHP shares were purchased by her father before 1985, her purchase cost is deemed to be the value of the shares when she inherited them ($6000). So, after the 50 per cent general discount she will be paying tax on a capital gain of $10 000. The NAB shares were purchased after 1985, so her purchase cost is the same as her father's, and the taxable capital gain on these shares after the discount is $14 000.

Capital gains tax issues are made easier when assets are owned by a discretionary trust, instead of by the person who died. In this situation, no change in ownership occurs as a result of the death, as the assets in the trust are not regarded as assets of the deceased.

CHAPTER 7

Fringe benefits tax

Fringe benefits tax (FBT) was introduced in 1986 to attack the perceived rorting of the tax system by highly paid employees. It was believed that employees were packaging their salaries to receive, before tax, benefits such as private school fees, golf club memberships, holidays and fully maintained cars.

Under the tax law existing at the time, this practice could have been attacked, but to do so would have meant investigating thousands of individual employees. The creation of the FBT system meant the onus of compliance was placed on employers—a much smaller number to police.

It wasn't until 1 April 1994 that FBT paid by employers became tax-deductible, with the result that the value of FBT benefits had to be grossed up by 1.9417 to arrive at their total taxable value. After the introduction of GST in 2000, a further change was made to account for the GST claimable by an employer, and resulted in an additional gross-up multiplier of 2.1292 being introduced.

At the time of writing there are still two gross-up multipliers. However, due to the top tax rate dropping from 48.5 per cent down to 46.5 per cent, the multipliers have also decreased. A fringe benefit that does not have GST included in its price has a multiplier of 1.8692; fringe benefits that have GST included in the price have a multiplier of 2.0647. So, for example, a fringe benefit of $1000 that included GST would have an FBT taxable value of $2065, with FBT of $960 payable.

When is FBT paid each year?

The FBT year finishes on March 31 each year, as opposed to the income tax year, which finishes on June 30. This means employers pay FBT tax on benefits provided to employees for the period from 1 April to 31 March. So, instead of being able to use the information prepared for income tax purposes, a separate calculation must be done for FBT.

What benefits are taxed?

To make the FBT system even more complicated, there are many types of benefits. Some result in tax being paid; others do not result in FBT being paid, but are still called 'fringe benefits'. Business owners can be caught in the FBT system either because of benefits they pay their employees, or because they are employees themselves for FBT purposes.

Note, however, that a business owner who is paid a wage, with PAYG withholding tax being deducted, will not necessarily be regarded as an employee for FBT. There is a legal principle that people cannot employ themselves, and this means that if a business is operated using a sole trader or partnership structure, the owners cannot technically be employees. When an owner cannot be classed as an employee, the benefits they receive will not be caught by the FBT system.

If a business is operated through a company or a trust, by contrast, benefits received by the business owners can be liable for FBT tax. For a benefit to be exempt from FBT, the owner/employee must have been paid a market salary and the benefit must not have been paid to any other employees. In other words, you have to be able to prove the benefit relates to ownership, not employment.

The FBT system was originally meant to apply only to benefits that employees obtained instead of earning taxable salary and wages. Over the years, though, the ATO has steadily increased the number of benefits that it regards as being caught in the FBT net. Not only are more and more specific benefits like cars and entertaining liable for FBT, any benefit obtained by an employee is also caught by a catch-all type of benefit called a 'residual benefit'.

Residual benefits are any benefit not covered by other specific sections of the FBT legislation. For a benefit to be classed as residual, there only needs to be a link between the benefit and a person's employment. This means the ATO can try and class almost anything as an FBT benefit; the tax office has tried to class numerous benefits that are not really related to employment as taxable fringe benefits. In some cases, these benefits are available to the general public — two examples were frequent flyer points earned from travel paid by employers, and credit card rewards earned from a business credit card.

This catch-all attitude on the part of the ATO, together with its increased audit activities focusing on employer obligations, mean employers should have a basic understanding of the main types of FBT benefits, and also what benefits are not taxable.

Car fringe benefits

The most common benefit received by employees under the FBT system is a car. There are two ways of calculating the

FBT taxable value for cars: the operating cost method and the statutory method.

Under the operating cost method, the total costs of maintaining a car for a year, including finance costs and depreciation, are calculated. This total is multiplied by the private use percentage of the vehicle, which is established by keeping a logbook for 12 weeks. The private use portion of the total costs of the car will be the taxable amount for FBT purposes.

The statutory method arrives at the taxable value with a lot less work, and is the most common method used. The taxable value is calculated by multiplying the cost of the car by a percentage based on the total number of kilometres driven in a year. The rates are as shown in table 7.1.

Table 7.1: fringe benefits tax rates on cars

Total kilometres driven in a year	FBT rate
Less than 15 000	26 per cent
15 000 to 24 999	20 per cent
25 000 to 39 999	11 per cent
40 000 and more	7 per cent

The kilometres-travelled figure used under this method is the total driven for a year, not just the business kilometres. A record of the number of kilometres travelled each year must be kept: if any of the required forms and documents cannot be produced in the event of a business being audited, the employer will pay FBT penalties. Also, under this system, if an employer relies on a declaration by an employee that proves to be wrong, the employer incurs the penalty.

Though it's the easiest and most common, the statutory method of paying FBT on cars doesn't always deliver the best after-tax result. Here are some rough guidelines that can indicate whether providing a car as a fringe benefit will be tax-effective. Where a car will have virtually no business kilometres, is purchased using a novated lease that costs less than $57 123, and will drive more than 25 000 kilometres a year, a tax benefit may be obtained by paying for the car using the FBT system. However, the higher the cost of the car, the lower the number of total kilometres driven a year, and the greater the percentage of business travel, the more likely it is that the FBT system should not be used to pay for the car.

Because FBT is paid on the grossed-up taxable value of the vehicle at the highest tax rate (at the time of writing 46.5 per cent), anyone who pays tax at a lower rate may be paying more tax than they need to if they are using the FBT system to pay for a car. This is an even more important consideration given that the 30 per cent tax rate will apply to taxable income up to $80 000 a year from 1 July 2008.

The FBT on motor vehicles may be minimised, however: once the taxable value of the car fringe benefit has been calculated, by the employee making a contribution. A contribution can be made by either paying directly for some of the running costs, such as petrol and repairs, or by reimbursing the employer for all or part of the taxable value.

Entertainment fringe benefits

After cars, the benefit most likely to be caught for FBT is entertaining. The tax office has laid down four tests to apply in defining what is taxable FBT entertaining. They are:

- why food and drink is being provided
- what is being provided
- when it is being provided
- where it is provided.

Examples of what would not be classed as meal entertainment include light refreshments provided on business premises during working hours, meals paid for when an employee is travelling overnight on business, and food and drink provided to employees attending a conference or training.

Where the food or drink is provided in the course of a recreation pursuit, by contrast, it *would* be classified as FBT taxable entertainment. 'Recreation' includes any activities done for amusement, such as sightseeing tours, sport or leisure activities like movies or golf, and any activities provided by means of a vehicle, ship, vessel or aircraft. Examples of taxable FBT meal entertainment provided to employees include business lunches, gifts of alcohol and food, tickets to sporting events or the movies, and the cost of a Christmas party or social function at a restaurant or function centre. For this last category, the taxable cost includes food or drink, travel and accommodation, venue hire and entertainment.

Only one type of Christmas party for employees has always been non-taxable—a party held on the business premises of the employer on a working day, and attended by current employees only. Where past employees or relatives attend, FBT is payable on the cost relating to them.

Not only do employers have to differentiate between entertaining and recreation, and whether the benefit is provided on business premises or other locations, the lavishness of the meal provided can also affect whether it would attract FBT. For example, sandwiches and fruit provided at work during a full day's training would not be classed as entertaining, but a seafood buffet supplied at a similar event may be.

When entertaining customers, the portion of the cost relating to an employee's meal is classed as a taxable fringe benefit. This means if you, as the owner/employee, entertain customers, the portion of the bill relating to your meal is caught for FBT.

There are three methods that can be used to calculate the benefit to employees when entertaining is done: the 50/50 method, the actual cost method, and by keeping a register for 12 weeks. This last option is similar to the logbook method for cars. A register must be kept for 12 weeks that establishes the percentage of entertaining that applies to employees. Once established, this percentage is used to calculate the liability relating to entertaining for FBT each year.

Under the 50/50 method, you assume that 50 per cent of all entertaining relates to employees. The actual cost method, by comparison, requires a lot of work. Every time entertaining is conducted, the cost must be apportioned between customers and employees on a per-head basis.

GST and income tax add a further complication to meals and entertaining. The percentage of entertaining subject to FBT is tax-deductible, and input tax credits can be claimed for it. The entertaining cost relating to customers, however, is not subject to FBT tax, is not tax-deductible, and no input tax credit can be claimed. Complexities like these mean you'd be wise, as a business owner, to have your activities reviewed by an accountant familiar with the legislation, to ensure you meet all your obligations.

Loan fringe benefits

Employers can also find themselves subject to FBT when trying to help out an employee in financial difficulty. If an employer provides any sort of loan benefit, such as paying an amount on behalf of an employee that is paid back over time, a value can be placed on the benefit that will be assessed for FBT.

This benefit could take the form of the interest that should have been charged on the loan, had it been done on commercial terms. It could also relate to fees and charges that would have been charged normally by a commercial lender, but have not been charged, such as application fees or discharge costs. Where an amount owed by an employee is forgiven, this is also a taxable fringe benefit.

Exempt fringe benefits

There are three main classes of benefits that may be exempt from FBT: benefits that fall under the 'otherwise deductible' rule, benefits that receive special treatment which effectively makes them exempt from FBT, and benefits that qualify for the minor fringe benefits exemption.

The 'otherwise deductible' rule

Under the 'otherwise deductible' rule, payments by an employer that would be tax-deductible to the employee are exempt from FBT. This covers such things as professional subscriptions or conference fees, but for the exemption to apply, the cost must be fully deductible to the employee. Where there is a private component, the 'otherwise deductible' exemption cannot apply to the full amount paid.

Benefits that receive other special treatment

There are a number of benefits that receive special treatment which effectively makes them exempt from FBT. These include:

- the provision of a mobile phone
- Qantas Club and similar airline membership fees
- a briefcase
- handheld computers, electronic organisers and PDAs
- laptop or notebook computers.

Apart from Qantas club membership and a briefcase, for benefits to be exempt the employer must be able to show they are used 'primarily' for business purposes. If this cannot be proven, all costs associated with them will be caught for FBT. For example, if the employee only phoned his or her spouse when running late occasionally, the phone would qualify as being used for primarily business purposes. If, however, the mobile was used constantly for private calls, the exemption would not apply.

Motor vehicles that have a carrying capacity of one tonne or more are also often regarded as being 100 per cent business use and thus exempt from FBT. To get this exemption, you must be able to prove that the private use of the vehicle is limited to travel from home to work and back, plus other minor, infrequent and irregular private travel. If the tax office can show that the private use of a vehicle is not minor or regular—say, if it's being used for shopping or going to the footy on weekends—all costs related to private use of the vehicle will be caught for FBT.

The minor fringe benefits exemption

To qualify for the minor fringe benefits exemption, a benefit must:

- be provided as a part of the employee's employment
- have a value of less than $300.

It must also be unreasonable of the ATO to treat it as a fringe benefit.

There are several matters that the ATO takes into consideration when determining if a benefit is minor and therefore exempt. These include:

- frequency and regularity
- cumulative value
- administrative difficulty
- circumstances of the benefit.

We'll look at each of these in a little more detail.

Frequency and regularity

Where a benefit is not regularly provided, and therefore is infrequent, it is more likely to be classed as minor. For example, a gift hamper given to employees every quarter would more than likely not qualify, but a hamper given on special occasions such as at Christmas or to celebrate the birth of a child would.

Cumulative value

The greater the total value of benefits provided over a year, the more likely they are not to qualify as minor. This means if an employer tries to beat the system by paying benefits that are just under the limit, and those benefits add up to a considerable amount, they would be less likely to be classed as minor.

Administrative difficulty

Where it would be difficult administratively for an employer to keep a record of the benefits provided, they are likely to be classed as minor.

Circumstances of the benefit

If the benefits can be seen to occur on special occasions or as a result of random generosity on behalf of the employer, instead of on a regular basis as part of rewarding employees, they are more likely to be considered minor.

Here's an example. Say that Rhett runs a restaurant. Over a year, he provides the following benefits to Scarlett, one of his waitresses:

- A gift to help her make a car payment when she ran out of money $285
- A bunch of flowers on her birthday $75
- A box of chocolates on Valentine's day $52
- Cost of her attending the staff Christmas party $180

As none of these benefits are over $300, and they are infrequent, they would more than likely be classed as exempt minor fringe benefits.

Minor fringe benefits and Christmas parties

Christmas parties may also be deemed a minor fringe benefit and exempt from FBT. This means an employer can spend up to $299 per person attending the Christmas party and still not be liable for FBT. This limit does, however, apply to all costs associated with the party, including the hire of a venue and the provision of food and drink for all those attending. To qualify for this exemption, too, the employer cannot use the 50/50 method for entertaining expenses.

Say that Nick Passage puts on a party for himself and his nine employees. He holds the party at the local pub and no expense is spared—the cost of hiring the function room, putting on a seafood buffet and supplying alcohol comes to $260 per head. In this case, no FBT tax is payable.

If, on the other hand, Nick also provided a band for the night at a cost of $500, the full cost would be $3100, or $310 per head. In this case, FBT tax of $2976 would be due. Also, under the old rules, had Nick given a Christmas hamper to all of his employees this cost would have also been caught. Fortunately the ATO has changed its view on this now: gifts given at a party are considered to be a separate benefit, and the $300 limit applies to them.

Where no FBT tax is payable, the cost of the party is not tax-deductible and no GST can be claimed. When FBT tax is payable, the cost of the party can be claimed as a tax deduction and the GST also claimed back.

CHAPTER 8

GST

The goods and services tax (GST) is now an integral part of Australia's taxation system. However, it is not a universal system (some goods and services are exempt from the tax), and so it is not a simple system. As a result, it's important that all business owners have a good working knowledge of their responsibilities regarding GST.

Under the relevant legislation, six elements must be satisfied before GST can be charged by a business on a transaction. They are:

- the entity must make a supply
- the supply must be for consideration
- the entity must be carrying on an enterprise
- the supply must be made in the course of the furtherance of that enterprise
- the supply must be connected with Australia
- the entity must be registered or required to be registered for GST purposes.

This is the legal basis for GST being charged. In plainer English, GST must be charged when a business (as opposed to a private person) supplies a good or service that will be used in Australia in exchange for money or something else of value, and the business is either registered or required to be registered for GST.

Under the legislation, a business must register for GST if its annual income is in excess of, or is going to exceed, $75 000. This figure does not include input-taxed goods or services. What follows are the other basic rules of the GST system. They have been simplified and, as such, are definitely only giving you the vibe of GST law and not the letter. Talk to your accountant for specifics regarding your situation.

Everyone pays GST

It doesn't matter whether you are an individual, a business, a church or a charity—everyone pays GST. The only way to avoid it is to not spend money, as every time a taxable good or service is supplied, GST is included in the price. The only transaction that escapes GST is when one unregistered private individual sells to, or does something for, another unregistered private individual.

GST is an exclusive system

Unless a good or service is specifically excluded under the GST legislation, it must have GST included in the price. The only two categories of goods and services that do not have GST charged on them are GST-free and input-taxed goods and services (which will be discussed a little later). If you do not sell or provide goods or services included in these categories, GST must be charged on everything your business provides.

When you must register for GST

All businesses that produce more than $75 000 a year in income must register for GST. Charities that earn more than $150000 in income a year must also register for GST. (Income from the supply of input-taxed goods and services is not included in these figures.) Businesses and charities that earn less than these income levels don't have to register for GST, but may choose to if they incur lots of expenses and want to be able to claim back the GST on them. If a business becomes aware that it will turn over more than $75000 a year, it must register for GST within 21 days. Income from the supply of input-taxed goods and services are not included in this income figure.

Most businesses do not effectively pay GST

All businesses pay GST on nearly everything they buy, and any GST paid by a registered business on a tax-deductible item can be claimed as a credit. This credit can then either be used to reduce the amount of GST that must be paid to the tax office, or be claimed as a refund, if the GST paid is greater than GST collected. Being able to claim a credit for GST paid means that businesses do not, in effect, pay GST.

For example, say a builder buys a door for $220. Included in the price is $20 of GST. When the builder later bills the homeowner $440 for installing and supplying the door, $40 of GST is included in the price. In this case, the builder has to send only $20 in GST to the tax office — the difference between the $40 of GST collected and the $20 of GST paid.

There are three main types of GST goods and services

The three types of GST goods and services are:

- GST-taxed
- GST-free
- input-taxed.

If something is not classed as GST-free or input-taxed, it must be GST-taxed. The necessities of life — such as unprocessed food, essential medical and health services and education — tend to be GST-free, along with goods and services that are exported. Input-taxed goods and services include financial services, such as bank interest and charges, and residential rental properties.

It does not matter what business structure you use

Where you fit into the GST system does not depend on how you operate your business — sole traders, partnerships, companies, co-operatives and trusts are all treated the same. It is the goods that you sell or the services you provide that dictate how you are treated under the GST system.

Two companies may have the same owners, yet one may have to charge GST and the other may not. An example of this would be two companies owned by a group of doctors, where one of the companies operates a medical practice and the other owns the building that the practice operates from. The company operating the medical practice would not charge GST to its patients on most of its income, while the property company would have to charge GST on the rent it collected.

Even an individual operating a business can provide a mixture of all three types of goods and services. For example, say a fruit retailer runs her business from a shop in a strip-shopping development. In addition to owning her building, she owns the building next door: the ground floor is rented to a hairdresser, while the residence upstairs is rented to a family. The income she generates from the fresh fruit she sells would be GST-free, the rent charged to the hairdresser would be GST-taxed, and the rent charged to the family would be input-taxed.

Who can claim GST as a refund is the main difference

The only factor that distinguishes businesses from un-registered consumers, and one business from another, is the ability to claim the GST paid as a refund. Registered businesses that sell or provide GST-taxed and GST-free goods and services can claim a credit for the GST they pay. Registered businesses that sell or provide input-taxed goods or services do not charge GST, and cannot claim a refund of the GST they pay. Any person or entity not registered must pay GST on all GST-taxed goods and services but cannot claim a refund.

As was evident in the fruit retailer example given earlier, a business can provide a combination of all three types of GST goods and services, and needs to account for each different sort of income and the costs incurred to produce that income. The fruit-shop owner, for example, would collect GST on the commercial rent and claim a credit for any GST on the costs she paid out in producing the rent. No GST would be collected on the fruit and vegetables sold, but a credit could be claimed for any GST paid on expenses like printing and stationery. On the residential rent no GST would be charged, and no credit could be claimed for any GST paid on costs associated with the house (plumbers' bills, for example).

How to register for GST

There are three ways in which you can register for GST. The first is to complete an Australian business number application form and mail it to the address given in the accompanying instruction booklet. The second is to have your tax agent or accountant complete the application for you and lodge it electronically. The last option is to complete an online application at <www.business.gov.au>.

What information is required?

The information to be completed on the application is relatively straightforward and does not require a lot of judgement. Section 1 asks for information to identify your business. Section 2 asks how you wish to be contacted. (One of these questions asks for the mailing address of your business—unless you're happy to deal with the tax office directly on matters and correspondence relating to GST, give the mailing address of your accountant.)

Section 3 gathers information that helps the tax office correctly classify your business for statistical purposes. Section 4 deals with information for new businesses, and has two questions relating to GST registration. The second-last question in this section asks if you are required to register for GST because of the total income of your business, and the last gives you the choice of registering for GST if you are not required to register.

Answers you need to think about

The GST section of the application has questions that are directly related to registering for GST. After the question which asks what the annual turnover of your business is, there are another two questions relating to how frequently you'd like to lodge your business activity statement. All three questions should be considered carefully. The turnover question is important, because various choices are offered to businesses that turn over less than $2 million and less than $20 million respectively. If your business turns over less than $20 million, you can choose to lodge your BAS, and paying your taxes, on a monthly or a quarterly basis.

For most businesses, where GST will be payable instead of producing a refund, you should choose to lodge quarterly. However, if you operate a business that provides GST-free goods or services (such as a medical practice), you should consider lodging monthly if your PAYG tax instalment is less than the GST refund. In these cases you will always get a refund of the GST you paid—helping your cash flow.

Businesses that turn over less than $2 million also have a choice between accounting for GST on a cash basis or an accruals basis. In just about every case you should choose the cash basis, as using this method you will only have to pay the GST you've actually collected. If you choose the accruals method your cash flow could be strained, because you may have to pay GST to the tax office on income that you've not yet collected.

Don't worry if you make a mistake

If you have completed and lodged your ABN application and made a wrong choice on the form, don't worry. If you chose the monthly option instead of the quarterly, listed your own address instead of your accountant's, or incorrectly applied to be registered for GST and you didn't need to, just ask the tax office to amend your application.

Accounting for GST

A business does not pay GST—it can offset any GST paid out against GST it has collected, or claim a refund. The ability to do this does not come without obligations, however. For starters, to be able to claim the credit, a business must be able to produce a tax invoice when asked for one by the tax office—meaning that every amount paid needs to be supported by a tax invoice.

Tax invoices

Below are the details required for an invoice to be a 'tax invoice' for GST purposes, where the invoice amount is $1000 or more. For an invoice of less than $1000, items 6, 7 and 9 are not required.

Details which must appear on a tax invoice:

1 the words 'tax invoice' stated prominently
2 the name of the entity selling the good or providing the service
3 the address of the supplier
4 the ABN of the supplier
5 the date of the invoice
6 the name of the customer or client
7 either the address of the customer/client or their ABN

8 a brief description of the goods or services supplied

9 the quantity of goods or the extent of services supplied

10 either the words 'total price includes GST' where GST is not separate amount, or the GST amount shown separately.

The importance of a good filing system

To ensure you can survive a GST audit by the ATO, you must have a good filing system. If you pay all business expenses by cheque, one good system is to file tax invoices and other supporting documentation in cheque number order. The alternative is to file tax invoices in alphabetical order according to the supplier's name. The main thing to remember is, if you cannot produce a tax invoice, you cannot claim a credit for GST paid.

Before you even start thinking about whether the best way to account for GST is using a manual system or a computer system, it is important that you are systematic when making payments. When cheques are written out, time can be saved if the amount of GST included on the tax invoice is shown on the cheque butt. This means you don't have to do calculations when recording the payments, and you'll account properly for items that don't have GST included in all of their value.

Manual bookkeeping

If you don't have a computer, a manual bookkeeping system needs to be in place to produce the revenue and expense information required to complete a BAS. The layout of a manual cashbook is fairly standard: a payments cashbook has columns for the date of the transaction, the name of the supplier, the cheque number, the amount paid, and GST. Following the GST column are a series of expense columns that have headings such as 'purchases', 'bank charges' and 'car costs'.

The secret of any manual bookkeeping system is being able to check the accuracy of the information recorded. To achieve this, each entry needs to be recorded at least twice, and three times when GST is included—first the total in the amount column, then the GST in the GST column, and the ex-GST amount in the relevant expense column. If the amounts have been recorded correctly, the total of the amount column should equal the total of the GST plus all of the expense columns.

A receipts cashbook is similar in layout, except it has the customer's name and receipt number instead of supplier and cheque number. After the amount column there's a GST column, then columns for different types of income and deposits.

Computer accounting

The easiest way to keep track of GST and the financial transactions of a business is using a computer accounting package. There's a wide choice of packages on the market: two of the most popular for small business are QuickBooks and MYOB. You can even get a program called Cashflow Manager that records payments and receipts in a manual cashbook format on computer.

From my experience, QuickBooks is the easiest to use of the computer packages available. It also has a handy feature that allows you to choose between the cash or accrual methods of accounting for reporting purposes. So, you might prepare your management accounts and income tax results using the accrual method but, if your business turns over less than $2 million a year, use the cash method for preparing the GST figures for the BAS.

Completing your BAS

Australia was the first country in the world to combine the reporting for all taxes on one form. The final version of the BAS was developed over many months after consultation with over three hundred accountants, large and small businesses and individual taxpayers.

The first page of a BAS has boxes for entering income and expense totals if you're using the 'actual method' of reporting. If you're using the annual method of reporting, the BAS will already list the amount the ATO advises you are required to pay.

The second page has a section for showing how much was paid in wages for the period, and how much PAYG withholding tax has been deducted. In addition, there is a section where you calculate how much PAYG instalments tax is payable. The middle section of the second page has boxes for the amount of GST collected and GST paid, plus boxes for the amounts owed for the PAYG taxes. In the final section, you enter how much you have to pay, or how much the ATO owes you.

Simplified reporting for GST

Food retailers such as milkbars, bakeries, sandwich shops and convenience stores that are registered for GST are eligible to use simplified methods, if:

- they sell both GST-free and GST-taxed goods from the same premises
- have a turnover of less than $2 million
- do not have point-of-sale equipment that can identify taxable and GST-free goods.

In all, three simplified accounting methods have been introduced so that small retailers are not forced to spend thousands on sophisticated point-of-sale equipment: the snapshot, stock purchases and business norms methods. The business's turnover and the type of food sold determines which of the three methods can be used.

Businesses that convert fresh food into prepared food, such as shops that make and sell sandwiches, have fewer choices than those that do not — greengrocers, for example. Food retailers that have a turnover of less than $1 million and do not convert food can choose between all three methods; businesses under the $1 million turnover limit that do convert food can only use the snapshot or business norms methods.

A business that does not convert food and has a turnover of between $1 million and $2 million may use either the snapshot method or the stock purchases method. Food retailers in the same turnover range that do convert food are limited to using the snapshot method.

The snapshot method

Under the snapshot method, a record must be kept of sales for a two-week period, and purchases for a four-week period, twice a year. For the July to December tax periods, the snapshot must be taken for a continuous period between

1 June and 31 July. For the January to June tax periods, the snapshot must be taken between 1 December and 31 January.

Sales need to be recorded on a worksheet that provides the total sales and the total GST-free sales each day. The percentage that GST-free sales make up of total sales for the two-week snapshot period can then be used to calculate GST-free sales for that six-month period. The purchases worksheet works the same way, except purchases are recorded over a four-week period.

The stock purchases method

Under the stock purchases method, purchases are recorded either continuously or for two four-week periods, just as with the snapshot method. Once the percentage of total purchases that GST-free purchases make up is established, it is used to calculate not only GST-free purchases but also GST-free sales for each period.

The business norms method

Under the business norms method, the tax office calculates standard percentages for GST-free sales and purchases, which are then used by retailers to calculate GST-free purchases and sales for each tax period. There are business norms available for:

- hot-bread shops
- convenience stores that do not prepare takeaway food or sell fuel or alcohol
- convenience stores that do prepare takeaway food but still do not sell fuel or alcohol

- fresh fish retailers
- rural convenience stores
- pharmacies
- cake shops
- health food shops
- delicatessens.

Timing differences between GST and income tax

There is one area in which, because of the complicated way the GST legislation is written, taxpayers can be disadvantaged. That area is real estate.

One real-estate-related complication arises because a transaction — the sale of a property — is treated one way for income tax but the opposite way for GST. Under income tax law, the sale of a property is regarded as taking place when there's a legally enforceable contract. This means capital gains tax or income tax is payable in the period the real estate is sold, instead of the period when the settlement takes place.

Let's look an an example. Fred signed a contract to sell a commercial property on 1 June 2007 for $330 000. Settlement takes place on 1 September 2007, and a capital gain of $50 000 is made. Under income tax law, the capital gain must be included on his 2007 tax return — not the 2008 return, when the settlement takes place.

The position for GST is the exact opposite where a standard contract is used. Under GST law, the sale of real estate is accounted for on the date of settlement or when the taxpayer takes possession of the property, not when the contract is signed. So, Fred would have to include the $30 000 of GST received on his September 2007 BAS, rather than his June BAS.

There is a further complication when a non-standard contract is used. Say Fred sold his property via a terms contract, under which the purchaser was to pay off the property over five years. He may need to pay the $30 000 of GST to the tax office by 28 October 2007, even though he may have only received $40 000 of the sale proceeds at that point in time.

The GST margin system for property

The margin scheme was introduced to the GST system to ensure that taxpayers registered for GST do not have to absorb the GST on the full selling price of property they owned on 1 July 2000, or property purchased after then that did not include GST. The scheme only applies to the sale of real property such as land, strata units and long-term leases.

Under this scheme, the GST payable on the sale of a property is one-eleventh of the difference between the selling price and the base value of the property. (Usually, GST is calculated as one-eleventh of the full selling value.) For property purchased after 1 July 2000, the base value is the price paid where no GST was included. For example, say a developer bought a block of land from a person not registered for GST in September 2006 for $70 000. The developer built a house that cost $150 000, and sold the house and land package in December 2007 for $270 000. As the cost of the land did not include GST, its base value under the margin scheme is $70 000. Using the margin scheme, therefore, the GST included in the selling value of $270 000 will be $18 182—one-eleventh of $200 000.

Property that was already owned at 1 July 2000 needs to be valued to establish its base value at that date. At first, the tax office rigidly applied its interpretation of the GST act, which meant that the valuation had to be carried out before the lodgement of the BAS relevant to the sale of the property. However, there is no section of the GST law that stipulates when the valuation must be done, and the tax office now recognises that there are circumstances in which a valuation cannot be obtained by the BAS lodgement date. In those circumstances, it allows more time for a valuation to be done—in effect, the Commissioner of Taxation has discretion as to when a valuation should be done.

GST and cars

Claiming motor vehicle costs for tax purposes has always been complicated. There are five different ways that car costs can be claimed, and there is a limit on the cost of cars when claiming depreciation. The introduction of the GST has added to the complexity. If business owners get it wrong, they may receive less money than expected when selling or trading in a vehicle.

When a GST-registered business sells an asset that has been used for business purposes, GST must be included in the price. So, if you were selling a work van and wanted to clear $13 000, you would have to sell it for $14 300 GST-inclusive. If this GST effect is not taken into account you will receive one-eleventh less for the vehicle being sold. In the case of the work van, only $11 818 would be received after the GST of $1182 was deducted.

Claiming a GST credit for cars

The amount of input tax credit you can claim on vehicles depends on several factors, the first being whether the vehicle is a car or a commercial vehicle (see page 160 for more). The full input tax credit is allowed for commercial vehicles, and this credit not only applies to the running costs of the vehicles, but also to the purchase cost. For example, if a delivery truck was purchased for $77000, a credit could be claimed for the $7000 of GST included in the price.

For cars, there is a limit on the amount of input tax credit claimable on the purchase cost — the depreciation cost limit, which at the time of writing was $57123. Where the GST-inclusive value of a car exceeds this limit, the maximum credit claimable is one-eleventh of the depreciation cost limit, thus $5182.

There is also a limit on the amount of input tax credits claimable on cars, on both the purchase cost and running costs, and this limit is based on the business use of the car. The percentage that can be claimed depends on which of the five methods for claiming car costs you are using. If you're using the set rate kilometre method, the amount of input tax credit you're allowed depends on the number of business kilometres that you can reasonably estimate you travel in a year. The percentages that can be claimed for total annual business kilometres are given in table 8.1.

Where you can reasonably estimate that your business travel is more than 5000 kilometres a year, and you use either the '12 per cent of original value' method or the 'one-third of total expenses' method, you can claim a third of the input tax credits. For example, under these methods, if the total GST paid on motor vehicle expenses were $300 for the quarter, you could claim an input tax credit of $100.

Table 8.1: GST credit claimable on cars

Total kilometres driven in a year	GST claimable
1 to 1250	5 per cent
1251 to 2500	10 per cent
2501 to 3750	15 per cent
3751 to 5000	20 per cent

If you are using the logbook method, you can claim the business use percentage of input tax credits for both the running costs and the purchase cost. For example, if you purchased a used car for $33 000 GST-inclusive, and you have a logbook that shows your business usage at 80 per cent, you could claim an input tax credit of $2400 (80 per cent of the $3000 of GST paid). In addition, you could claim 80 per cent of all of the GST included in running costs such as fuel, repairs and tires.

If you're using the fringe benefits tax system to claim motor vehicle costs, you can claim 100 per cent of the GST in the running costs and the purchase cost up to the depreciation cost limit.

The GST traps of car finance

The GST has made the decision of how to best finance the purchase of a car much more complicated. Depending on how your business accounts for GST, and what type of finance is used, the cash flow of the business can be hurt, due to an unexpected GST bill. (For information on how car finance can affect other kinds of tax, see chapter 11.)

After you've sorted out what's the best car to buy, not what gives the best tax deduction, it's time to decide what's the best type of finance to use. Where a car will be kept for the full term of the finance contract, a lease should be used. A lease is easier to account for, and the after-tax cost of the lease is only very slightly more than the other forms of finance.

If there is a chance that a car may be sold before the finance contract expires, a hire-purchase or chattel mortgage should be used. If your business accounts for the GST using the accrual method, there is very little difference between hire-purchase and a chattel mortgage. Under the accrual method, income and expenses are accounted for when they are earned or incurred. As a result, the GST paid on the purchase price can be claimed in full in the period the car is purchased.

If your business uses the cash method of accounting, however, the choice between the two forms of finance is more critical. The cash method only allows you to claim a credit for GST paid out, so if hire-purchase is used, the GST can only be claimed on a proportional basis. In other words, the value of the GST credit is claimable over the term of the contract. Where a chattel mortgage is used, on the other hand, the tax office has ruled that a business using the cash method can claim the GST paid in full in the period of purchase.

The best way to illustrate the effect of each finance method for a business using the cash method is via an example. Say that a plumber needed to replace his old van, and purchased a new van for $33 000. A trade-in of $11 000 was negotiated for the old van, and the balance of $22 000 was financed by a hire-purchase contract. The contract was taken out for a period of four years and only one monthly payment had been made by the end of the quarter.

When preparing his next BAS, the plumber found that $1000 of the trade-in he received had to be included as GST received. But because a four-year hire-purchase contract was used, only a forty-eighth of the $3000 in GST paid could be claimed. This meant the plumber had to pay the difference between the $1000 of GST collected and the $63 of GST claimable. For every subsequent quarter until the contract finishes, he can make a claim for $188 of GST credit.

If the plumber had instead used a chattel mortgage to finance the purchase, a net GST credit of $2000 could have been claimed, made up of the $3000 GST credit minus the $1000 in GST collected on the trade-in.

To ensure that the best form of finance is obtained when you're purchasing a new car, the financing should be regarded as a different undertaking, not part of the purchase. A good way of approaching this is to tell the salesperson that any finance deal proposed will be compared with a finance deal offered by an independent broker. This can be important, because some finance companies linked to car dealerships do not offer chattel mortgage finance. It's important to shop around.

Most finance brokers can ensure that not only are you getting a good interest rate, you are also getting the best type of finance for your needs. For example, some contracts allow the GST to be paid in a one-off special repayment that reduces the monthly repayments.

GST on the sale of a business

The selling of a business asset, or the selling of a business itself, are two activities regarding which business owners need to understand their GST obligations. In some cases GST will need to be charged, while in others no GST will apply. It depends on whether the asset fits into one of two GST-free categories:

- farming land
- an asset that forms part of the sale of a going concern.

Farming land

There are two different situations in which farming land is classed as GST-free. The first is where farming land is sold to an associate of the vendor. To be classed as GST-free in this case, the land must have been used in a farming business for at least five years, the selling value to the associate must be either nil or less than the GST-inclusive market value, and the land must be potential residential land. This exemption was introduced to avoid GST being charged on land that is passed from one generation to the next, or within families. It applies even when the land is not going to be used for farming, but for, say, building a house.

The second situation in which the sale of farming land will be GST-free is when the land being sold was used for at least five years for a farming business and the purchaser of the land intends to carry on a farming business on the land.

The term 'farming business' can include:

- growing plants or other crops
- maintaining animals for sale or for selling something they produce (like wool)
- manufacturing dairy produce from milk produced by the owner
- planting and tending trees for the purpose of harvesting them.

The sale of a going concern

Under the second GST-free category, the asset being sold must be part of the sale of a going concern. To qualify under the 'going concern' provisions, both the vendor and the purchaser must be registered, or be required to be registered, for GST. In addition, the asset being sold must be subject to an agreement in writing that states that it is being sold as part of a going concern, and the vendor must both include everything required by the purchaser to carry on a business, and carry on the business right up to the point when the asset is sold.

The following example will help explain these conditions. Say that Adam sells his retail lawnmower business to Eve. Included in the contract of sale is the goodwill of the business, stock, and all of the equipment and fittings needed to carry on the business. In addition, the lease of the shop is transferred to Eve. Eve registers for GST before taking over the business, and Adam carries on the business until Eve takes it over. In this case, no GST needs to be included in the selling price.

When GST must be paid

When the asset being sold does not fit either of the GST-free criteria, and the vendor is registered for GST, GST must be included in the selling value. If the purchaser is also registered and is going to use the asset as part of a business, it shouldn't matter that GST is charged, as he or she will be able to claim a credit for it.

If the purchaser is not registered for GST, however, such as where farming land is purchased to build a house, the GST charged could disadvantage both the vendor and the purchaser. The vendor may have to give some of the selling value to the tax office as GST; the purchaser may end up paying more than he or she had intended to. Where a purchaser is not registered for GST the margin method for calculating GST should be used.

CHAPTER 9

State and territory business taxes

When you own a business, you must pay taxes to many layers of government. At the top of the tree is the federal government, followed by the state or territory government, and at the grass-roots level is local government.

As we saw in the section in chapter 5 about dealing with employees' issues, the middle level of government imposes taxes on employers in the form of workers compensation insurance. The bad news is, this is not the only way that state and territory governments raise revenue from businesses: they also impose payroll tax and, except in the Northern Territory, charge land tax.

Payroll tax

It is a common misconception that payroll tax tends to be mainly paid by large businesses, not small businesses. Payroll tax is payable whenever an employer's total for salary and wages exceeds a threshold; and it's the employer's responsibility to register for payroll tax and start paying it. As you can see from the thresholds detailed in table 9.1, overleaf, in some states reasonably small businesses pay payroll tax.

The threshold acts as a tax-free amount for salaries: the payroll tax rate is only applied to the salaries and wages that exceed the threshold.

Table 9.1: payroll tax thresholds in states and territories

State or territory	Yearly payroll threshold	Rate
ACT	$800 000	6.85 per cent
New South Wales	$600 000	6.00 per cent
Northern Territory	$1 250 000	6.20 per cent
Queensland	$1 000 000	4.75 per cent
South Australia	$504 000	5.25 per cent
Tasmania	$1 010 000	6.10 per cent
Victoria	$550 000	5.05 per cent
Western Australia	$750 000	5.50 per cent

Just as there are grouping provisions in some WorkCover legislation, there are also grouping provisions for payroll tax. This effectively means a business cannot escape payroll tax by setting up different entities so the payroll for each entity is below the threshold. Indeed, the grouping provisions legislation is so broad it can cause entities to be grouped even where there is no common ownership.

Along with mistakes involving the grouping provisions, a common error found in payroll tax audits is not including payments to certain contractors as remuneration subject to payroll tax. As is the case for WorkCover, payments to any type of contractor can form part of taxable remuneration for payroll tax purposes, the only exceptions being when specific legislation excludes a payment.

Another common mistake is a failure to aggregate the wages of an employer — group or otherwise — that employs people in several states. Under the relevant legislation, if an employer is liable for payroll tax in one state, it will be liable for payroll tax in the other states, even if the total for wages in the other states are below the relevant thresholds.

For example, say that a furniture removal company has its headquarters in Victoria, but also has warehouse and sales staff in Queensland and New South Wales. The total the company pays for salaries and wages in Victoria is $1 million. In Queensland, the payroll totals $150 000, and in New South Wales it is $200 000. Under the aggregation rules payroll tax is payable in all three states.

If you think that the chances of being discovered are slim, think again — the revenue authorities in each of the states and territories exchange information fairly freely.

Land tax

If there was ever a tax that could be scrapped or overhauled on the basis of how complicated it is and how markedly it differs depending on where you live, it's land tax. In this section, I will try to give a general overview of how it works.

Land tax is levied by each state and the ACT on the value of nearly all the land owned within its borders. It is paid by all entities including individuals, trusts and companies. Where trusts own land that cannot be attributed to an individual, special, higher rates apply.

The exemptions to land tax include:

- a person's principal place of residence
- land used for primary production
- retirement villages, aged-care establishments and nursing homes.

There are also exemption for land owned by religious and charitable institutions and other non-profit organisations.

In New South Wales, land used and occupied primarily for boarding houses is also exempt, along with certain property used for low-cost accommodation within a five-kilometre radius of Sydney.

The land value used to calculate land tax is the 'unimproved' value — the method of valuation differs between the states. Table 9.2 shows the different valuation methods used, as detailed on each taxing authority's website.

Table 9.2: land valuation methods for land tax

State or territory	Land value method
ACT	Value as defined in section 9 of the *Land Tax Act 2004*
New South Wales	Valuer-General valuation as at 1 July preceding each land tax year
Queensland	Department of Natural Resources and Water valuation done in March each year
South Australia	Value of land at midnight each June 30
Tasmania	Valuer-General determines value on a periodic basis
Victoria	Local council valuation every two years
Western Australia	Valuer-General determines value on an annual basis

As valuers can sometimes get it wrong, it is important that if you receive a land tax notice with a new valuation, you check it for reasonableness. If it appears too high, each state and the ACT allow a period for you to object against the valuation. If you do not object within the time allowed, and the valuation is too high, it's your bad luck — and you still have to pay the tax on the higher value.

If you own land that is subject to land tax, it is your responsibility to register with the relevant authority. If you don't register within the required time frame, and the taxing authority finds you are liable for land tax, penalties will be imposed.

Be aware that just because you don't own the property you operate your business from doesn't mean you won't be paying land tax. In most cases, leases for commercial property make the tenant liable for all costs and taxes related to the rented premises. This means you, as the tenant, must pay costs such as council rates, body corporate levies, water rates and land tax.

You can also end up paying land tax because the previous owner did not pay the tax they should have. Each taxing authority has a system that allows purchasers of property to be advised if there is any outstanding land tax relating to the property. This enables the purchaser to adjust the amount they pay the vendor to take account of the outstanding land tax. Once a certificate has been supplied giving the amount of tax outstanding, a taxing authority cannot come back in the future to demand tax owing by a previous owner.

The actual rates for land tax differ greatly. New South Wales has one of the simplest methods for charging the tax: it is paid for the 2007–08 year on all applicable land where the combined value exceeds $359 000, at the rate of 1.6 per cent of the value in excess of the threshold, plus a fee of $100. The land tax rates for the other states and the ACT are given in tables 9.3 to 9.8, on the following pages.

Table 9.3: Australian Capital Territory land tax

Residential properties

Land value threshold	Rate
Up to $75 000	0.6 per cent of value over $0
$75 001 to $150 000	$450 plus 0.89 per cent of value over $75 000
$150 001 to $275 000	$1117.50 plus 1.15 per cent of value over $350 000
$275 001 and over	$3205 plus 1.4 per cent of value over $275 000

Commercial properties

Land value threshold	Rate
Up to $150 000	0.89 per cent of value over $0
$150 001 to $275 000	$1335 plus 1.25 per cent of value over $150 000
$275 001 and over	$2897.50 plus 1.59 per cent of value over $275 000

The ACT uses an average unimproved value for the purposes of calculating land tax.

Table 9.4: Queensland land tax

Land value threshold	Rate
$0 to $599 999	Nil
$600 000 to $749 999	$1200 plus 0.7 per cent of value over $599 999
$750 000 to $1 249 999	$2250 plus 1.45 per cent of value over $749 999
$1 250 000 to $1 999 999	$9500 plus 1.5 per cent of value over $1 249 999
$2 000 000 to $2 999 999	$20 750 plus 1.675 per cent of value over $1 999 999
$3 000 000 and above	1.25 per cent of taxable value

In Queensland, where property values increase dramatically from one year to the next, a 50 per cent cap has been put on how much the previous year's value can increase by. This cap does not apply to subdivided land.

Table 9.5: South Australian land tax

Land value threshold	Rate
Up to $110 000	Nil
$110 001 to $350 000	0.3 per cent of value over $110 000
$350 001 to $550 000	$720 plus 0.7 per cent of value over $350 000
$550 001 to $750 000	$2120 plus 1.67 per cent of value over $550 000
$750 001 to $1 000 000	$5420 plus 2.4 per cent of value over $750 000
Over $1 000 000	$11 420 plus 3.7 per cent of value over $1 000 000

Table 9.6: Tasmanian land tax

Land value threshold	Rate
Less than $25 000	Nil
$25 000 to $349 999	$50 plus 0.55 per cent of value over $25 000
$350 000 to $749 999	$1837.50 plus 2.00 per cent of value over $349 999
$750 000 and over	$9837.50 plus 2.5 per cent of value over $749 999
$2 000 000 to $2 999 999	$20 750 plus 1.675 per cent of value over $1 999 999

Table 9.7: Victorian land tax

Land value threshold	Rate
Less than $225 000	Nil
$225 000 to $539 999	$250 plus 0.2 per cent of value over $225 000
$540 000 to $899 999	$880 plus 0.5 per cent of value over $540 000
$900 000 to $1 619 999	$2680 plus 0.8 per cent of value over $900 000
$1 620 000 to $2 699 999	$8440 plus 1.3 per cent of value over $1 620 000
$2 700 000 and over	$22 480 plus 2.5 per cent of value over $2 700 000

Table 9.8: Western Australian land tax

Land value threshold	Rate
Up to $250 000	Nil
$250 001 to $875 000	0.15 per cent of value over $250 000
$875 001 to $2 000 000	$937.50 plus 0.75 per cent of a value over $875 000
$2 000 001 to $5 000 000	$9375 plus 1.3 per cent of value over $2 000 000
$5 000 001 to $10 000 000	$48 375 plus 1.55 per cent of value over $5 000 000
$10 000 001 and over	$125 875 plus 2.3 per cent of value over $10 000 000

CHAPTER 10

Tax planning tips

In chapter 1 of this book I said that to avoid tax is wrong. I also said that where possible Australians can and should be involved in tax planning so they do not pay more tax than they have to. This chapter covers some basic areas of tax planning open to both business owners and employees.

The first thing to understand is that tax planning is mainly about delaying paying tax, not about actually saving tax. The principle at work in tax planning is that it is always best to delay paying for something for as long as possible, and when that something is tax, the longer the better.

There *are* times when tax is actually saved, but these are rare. One of the few tax-planning measures that delivers a tax saving is superannuation; tax savings can also happen when you delay earning income and there is a decrease in tax rates or a change in tax thresholds.

Nevertheless, there have been many tax schemes over the years that have promised huge tax savings. Some of these were out-and-out tax avoidance that made the promoters lots of money and landed the taxpayers in a heap of trouble with the ATO. Others were merely totally mismanaged — resulting in taxpayers getting a reduction in tax because they lost all of their money!

In the end, when it comes to tax planning it's always better to end up with 53.5 per cent of something (the percentage you are left with after paying tax at the top rate), than 100 per cent of nothing.

End-of-year tax planning

At the end of each financial year, there is a mad scramble by people in business to try and reduce their payable tax. Frequently, this is done very close to 30 June, and when things are done in a rush often very little in the way of a tax saving is achieved.

A much smarter approach is to estimate well in advance of 30 June what your taxable income for the year will be. The most accurate way of doing this is to provide information to your accountant and ask him or her to estimate your tax liability. For those people who want to save money, however, the information accumulated when complying with the GST reporting requirements can be used.

Where a simple cashbook has been used, it should be relatively easy to calculate what profit has been made for the year. This is, however, not the total amounts banked less the total payments—included in the payments may be amounts that are not fully tax-deductible. For example, businesses do not get a full tax deduction for the cost of plant and equipment: only a portion of the cost will be allowed as a depreciation deduction. And the amounts repaid on a loan during the year will consist of both principal and interest (unless it is an interest-only loan). The interest component will be tax-deductible but the principal amount won't.

Where a computer accounting package has been used to prepare GST returns, a profit and loss statement should be easy to generate. However, just as the figures from a cashbook should be adjusted, the amounts given in a profit and loss statement should also be reviewed to ensure only deductible costs are included.

It is also vital to review all the items that appear on the balance sheet produced by the accounting system, to ensure they are all correct. Most mistakes in a balance sheet translate into either more or less taxable profit. Some of the most obvious items to check are the amounts shown for bank accounts, accounts receivable, stock, accounts payable and loan balances with banks and other financial institutions.

After all adjustments and checks have been made, the interim profit must then be reduced by an estimate of the depreciation deduction for that year. The depreciation amount shown in the previous year's tax return can be used for this purpose.

The resulting estimated interim profit or loss figure will indicate whether there will be a tax problem. If a large capital profit has been made, or there has been a major increase in business profits, tax may be payable at one of the two top marginal tax rates. But before you embarking on more radical ways of saving tax, there are a number of strategies that can help reduce your business profit. We'll look at each of these in turn over the following pages.

Writing off bad debts

To be able to write off a debt as bad, and therefore not pay tax on revenue you will never collect, it must be removed from debtors/accounts receivable before June 30 each year.

This means you should carefully review your debtors before then, identify the debtors that will not pay and write them off. You must be able to show that any debt written off is uncollectible, and that you have made every effort to try to collect it.

Delaying capital gains

If you are contemplating selling an asset that will produce a capital gain, the very least you should do, if possible, is delay the sale until after June. This will put the taxable capital gain into the next year, and will mean you won't be paying tax on the gain until December of the following tax year, at the earliest.

Creating capital losses

If you've made a capital gain through the year, you should review your investments to identify any that decreased in value below what you paid for them. If those investments are sold before June 30, the capital loss will decrease the capital gains you made during the year. If the investment you sell is expected to increase in value, you can always buy it back — though make sure to factor in the buy and sell costs, to make sure they do not exceed any tax that will be saved.

Carrying out repairs

Repairs to business premises, plant and equipment and motor vehicles are fully tax-deductible. If repairs are carried out in July or August, the tax reduction will not be enjoyed until after the end of that tax year, so it makes sense to carry out repairs or maintenance in May or June. This consequent tax deduction will result in a tax saving almost immediately.

Delaying income

During June, you can decrease your tax payable by not invoicing or billing for goods supplied or services rendered until July. This can be important if you have a customer who may not pay you for 90 or 120 days. By delaying earning that income, you reduce the profit for that year. Care should be taken when using this strategy, however, as it can decrease the cash flow of your business.

Paying employee superannuation

Superannuation contributions are treated the same way under both the cash and the accrual methods of accounting: tax legislation dictates that a tax deduction can only be claimed for superannuation actually paid. It therefore makes sense to pay all superannuation contributions required for employees by June 30, so that the tax deduction can be claimed in the same year.

Reviewing motor vehicles

You should review the way you are claiming motor vehicle expenses, to ensure that you're maximising your deduction. If you chose the logbook method, check to see when the logbook was kept. If the logbook was maintained five years ago, you'll need to keep a new one (see chapter 11 for more details).

Reviewing fixed assets

A review should be done of the assets shown on the business's depreciation schedule. Any assets that have been scrapped should be written out of the schedule and their written-down value claimed as a tax deduction, and any assets not used any more should be scrapped and claimed likewise.

Prepaying expenses

As mentioned in chapter 3, if you are an SBE you can prepay up to 13 months of a deductible expense. Costs that are often prepaid include lease payments, interest, rent, professional services, hire of plant and equipment, advertising and consumables such as printing and stationery.

Purchasing new equipment that costs under $1000

If you are an SBE, and you know that you'll need to either replace or buy new equipment that costs less than $1000, do it just before 30 June so that you'll receive a tax deduction for the full amount paid.

Recognising work done by children

Another actual tax saving can be obtained where children of the owners work in the business. Children under 18 pay tax at the highest rate on profits above $416 that are distributed to them from a business. Where they earn a wage for work done, however, they are treated like an adult taxpayer.

Too often, when children work in a small business the parents pay them for their efforts from their own pockets. Instead of doing this, the arrangements should be formalised, just as they are with other employees. An employee declaration should be completed, proper records kept of the time worked, and wages paid with tax deducted where applicable. If you have children who have worked in your business during the year, and you can demonstrate this, they should be paid a wage before June 30 to recognise the work done.

Reviewing shareholder loans

If your business is operated through a company, a check should be made for any shareholder or director's loan accounts. It is quite common for shareholder/owners to take money out of the business during the year over and above any salary paid, and where these drawings exceed the amount owed to them a potential tax problem can arise.

Because of the low tax rate paid by companies, tax laws exist to ensure shareholder/owners cannot gain an unfair advantage. It would be inequitable for sole traders to pay tax at 46.5 per cent on part of their business profit, while shareholders pays tax at only 30 per cent but can use all of the profit for their own personal benefit.

Where shareholders owe the company money, they must pay interest on the loan at a benchmarked interest rate and repay the loan over a commercially applicable period. If the loan is unsecured, it must be repaid in seven years; if it is secured by a registered charge over an asset, such as a home, it can be repaid over 25 years.

Where no repayments are made and no interest is charged, the loan can be deemed an unfranked dividend, and in this situation the shareholder pays tax at their marginal rate of tax, without a credit for tax paid by the company. If you find yourself in this position, contact your accountant, as shareholder loans can be repaid in various ways without causing any financial hardship for the shareholder. One strategy is to pay fully franked dividends to the shareholders.

Contributing to superannuation

The most tax-effective action a business owner can take before June 30 is to ensure he or she has made the maximum allowable super contribution. Superannuation is one of the few end-of-year measures where an actual tax saving can be achieved. For the 2008–09 year, the maximum deductible contribution is $50 000 if you are under 50, and $100 000 if you are 50 or over.

Revaluing trading stock

When placing a value on your stock at hand at the end of the year, you should take note of any slow-moving or damaged stock. The higher the value of your stock, the more profit you make and the more tax you pay — and the tax office allows you to value stock at the lower of cost or net realisable value. So if a stock item will have to be sold for less than it cost, you can value it at this lower selling price, thus recognising the loss you will make.

The trap of buying new equipment

One tactic employed by business owners with a tax problem is to purchase a new car or a new piece of machinery. The problem is, by doing this in June you decrease the cash reserves of your business without decreasing the profit by any worthwhile amount. Businesses classed as an SBE at least get half of what would normally be claimed for a full year; those not classed as an SBE get very little at all.

If an asset is purchased on 23 June at a cost of $20 000, and has a yearly depreciation claim of $4000, the deduction for the year it was purchased would be approximately $80. This is because you will only get a deduction for a week's depreciation, not for a full year's depreciation, and definitely not for the full cost of the asset purchased.

It's important here to understand one of the underlying principles of accounting and tax: that the profit of a business is arrived at by deducting from the income all of the *expenses paid so that the income could be earned*. So, when you buy an asset in June, you only get a claim for its depreciation during the period you owned it.

The cost of assets is written off as depreciation over their estimated effective useful life. If you purchase a machine that will produce a product for an estimated five years, its cost is written off as a depreciation deduction over that five-year period. If you could claim the full cost of the asset in the first year, the profits in that year would be unfairly reduced.

Sometimes there can be a difference between the rate of depreciation used for tax and the rate used for accounting: it may come as a surprise that in most cases you get a more generous deduction under taxation rules than you do under strict accounting principles. For example, say that a farmer pays $21 000 to have a dam dug to help conserve and collect water. If the dam has an effective life of 20 years, the accounting depreciation would be $1050 a year. Under tax rules, that dam could be written off in three equal instalments, resulting in a tax deduction of $7000 in the first year.

Don't pay cash for assets

If you need to buy a new asset just before 30 June, you should consider financing the purchase. In fact, as I've mentioned before, as a general principle you should not pay cash for an asset—it can be better to finance the purchase over the time period you expect to asset to last.

There are four ways in which you can purchase an asset: you can pay cash, or finance the purchase using hire-purchase, a loan or a lease. If you do not finance the purchase, your cash profit will be tied up in an asset while you only get a tax deduction for the depreciation. It makes a lot more sense to finance the purchase and use the excess cash to increase your super contribution or prepay an expense.

If you decide to use hire-purchase or a loan, you will get a deduction for the interest component of the finance and also get a deduction for depreciation. The difference between a loan and hire-purchase is that with a loan you normally have to put up other property as security. Hire-purchase finance also normally takes less time to organise than a loan does. However, one benefit a loan can have over hire-purchase is that if you are an SBE you can prepay the interest for up to 13 months, thus increasing your deduction for the year.

The most tax-effective of all the options can be leasing the asset. As with the loan, you can prepay up to 13 months of lease payments, and because lease payments have both a principal and an interest component, they will usually give you the biggest tax deduction.

Table 10.1 shows the different tax deductions achieved for a piece of equipment purchased on 1 June 2008 for $30 000, and that has a depreciation rate of $6000 per year. The interest rate used for the finance options is 8.5 per cent, with the term for the finance being five years.

From the table it is obvious that the best tax deduction is generated by the lease option. However, keep in mind that the same tax deduction can be achieved for all three finance options if the cash not tied up in the asset is used to fund a deductible super contribution for the owner.

Table 10.1: payment options for business assets

Purchase option	Cash paid	Dep'n	Deductions Interest	Lease	Total ded'n
Cash	$30 000	$500			$500
Hire-purchase	$615	$500	$115		$615
Loan interest prepaid	$1995	$500	$1495		$1995
Lease prepaid	$7995			$7995	$7995

The best option for you will depend on your particular circumstances. It is always advisable when you have to make these decisions to get help from your accountant; they should not only be able to help you make the right decision, but may also be able to find a cheaper source of finance.

Gearing and tax

The term 'gearing' can mean different things to different people. For some, when it is combined with the word 'negative', it is as a tax-avoidance scheme blamed for many of the excesses of the recent property boom. In a business and investment sense, however, 'gearing' is only another name for borrowing.

Under current tax law, when you borrow for an income-producing purpose the interest is tax-deductible. This applies to loans taken out to purchase property, shares, plant and equipment, or a business. There is nothing special about the tax deductibility of interest: for many investors and business people it is just another cost.

Part of the reason why negative gearing has got such a bad name is a few developers who promote the purchase of properties on the tax benefits instead of their investment benefits. Investors who have been enticed into buying a property purely for the tax benefits may find that they have paid too much and the investment never makes a real profit.

Often developers try to suck in new investors by claiming they have unearthed some little-known tax law that means an investor's tax benefit will help pay for the property. Let me repeat: there is nothing special about the ability to reduce tax. The main tax benefit from a negatively geared property comes because the tax loss is often greater than the cash loss. The higher the tax rate an individual pays, the greater the tax benefit of a negative gearing loss.

Table 10.2, overleaf, shows the difference between a cash loss and a tax loss, and the effect that a person's tax rate has on the tax reduction. It also compares the tax savings and net cash cost, for each of the tax rates, between borrowing $300 000 to invest in property and the same amount to invest in shares.

Table 10.2: the impact of negative gearing

	$	15 per cent $	30 per cent $	40 per cent $	45 per cent $
PROPERTY					
Rent	15 000				
Less interest	21 000				
Less rates	1500				
Less insurance	500				
Less sundry	1000				
	24 000				
Cash loss	9000	9000	9000	9000	9000
Depreciation	2500				
Building write-off	3750				
Tax loss	**15 250**				
Less tax saving		2288	4575	6100	6863
Net cash loss		**6713**	**4425**	**2900**	**2138**
DIRECT SHARES					
Dividends	12 000				
Less interest	21 000				
Cash loss	9000	9000	9000	9000	9000
Less franking credit	5143				
Tax loss	3857				
Less franking credit		5143	5143	5143	5143
Less tax saving		579	1157	1543	1736
Net cash loss		**3278**	**2700**	**2314**	**2121**

Assumptions:
Cost of house and share portfolio $300 000.
Only interest paid on loan at 7 per cent, no principal repayments.

When the imputation franking credits are taken into account (these act as an extra amount of tax paid on behalf of the investor), on a $300 000 investment in shares the net cash loss is less than an investment in property for all investors.

The table also shows that there can be a difference between the negative gearing cash loss and the tax loss claimable. For shares, the franking credits increase their tax-effectiveness and thus reduce the cash loss. For property, a tax deduction is allowed for non-cash costs such as the depreciation of fixtures and fittings (including carpets, ovens and hot-water services), and the cost of constructing the building.

The special deduction for the construction costs of residential buildings was introduced in 1985 for buildings constructed after 18 July 1985. Originally the deduction was 4 per cent of the construction costs, but this decreased to 2.5 per cent for buildings constructed after 15 September 1987. Until 1997, however, the tax deduction for construction costs did not decrease the cost of the property for capital gains tax purposes. This changed in the 1997 Federal Budget: the cost base for capital gains tax of properties purchased after 13 May 1997 is decreased by the amount of any tax deductions claimed for construction costs.

Growing an investment with tax savings

Agribusiness investments have come a long way from when they first came to prominence in the 1980s. Back then they were called 'afforestation projects', while today the more mainstream investments are known as forestry or horticultural managed investment schemes. One of the main attractions of these investments, then and now, is that you may be able to claim a tax deduction for the amount invested.

Agricultural projects were two of the most popular tax-effective investments in the 1990s, along with film schemes. In the film scheme category, very few people other than the promoters and the filmmakers made any money. The agricultural projects have been many and varied: in most cases the exotic projects, such as ostriches, wildflowers and nashi pears, reduced tax at the expense of the investors losing their money! The other type of agricultural project, however, was in more established areas such as forestry investments in blue gum and pine plantations. These projects have proved themselves commercially viable overseas in such places as New Zealand. The problem is, many people who invested in these types of projects during the late 1980s also lost their money.

I must admit to being one such investor. Nonetheless, my bad experience with a pine plantation investment did not deter me, and I have invested in other projects, including blue gums and pine trees, since my first failed venture. To understand why I believe these types of investments do have a place in an investment portfolio, it is important to understand why the earlier schemes failed.

The three main contributing factors were greed, incompetence and tax minimisation at any cost. Many of the early pine projects, for example, were sold at a time when the highest marginal tax rate was between 49 per cent and 60 per cent. This drove some people to invest in schemes just to decrease tax. As I've said before, the prime consideration for any investment should be its commercial viability, and tax should be secondary.

The greed was contributed equally by the managers, sellers and buyers of the projects. The buyers' greed related to the desire to save tax at any cost; the sellers were attracted to the huge commissions paid by the managers; and the managers loved the huge profits they could make by charging inflated costs for establishing the plantations.

The incompetence was purely on the part of the managers. In a lot of the early investments, the managers' main source of income was the upfront establishment costs. This meant when the tax laws were tightened to restrict tax deductions, and the recession began, the number of people investing in the forest projects dropped dramatically. With no significant recurring source of income, many managers failed.

Back when I invested in my first project, it made sense to me on stand-alone investment principles as well as for saving tax. It was clear that the rate at which we were cutting down our native forests was not sustainable. It was also clear that Australia's demand for wood and paper products would continue to increase. This led me to believe that a well-run commercial plantation should be commercially viable long term.

This belief has only been strengthened over recent years. The two main contributors to this increased optimism have been how the agribusiness investment industry has evolved and how the federal government has gone from a combative approach to the industry to one that is actually supportive.

The industry has gone from being many small privately owned businesses, driven by tax savings, to professionally managed public companies whose projects are assessed by independent rating agencies. And in recent times the government has, after consulting with the industry, provided certainty for investors by announcing it will pass legislation locking in tax deductions for approved forestry projects. One of the criteria requires that the manager of the project spend at least 70 per cent of the funds raised on growing the trees, which should also increase the chances of the projects being profitable.

One of the biggest impediments to people investing in forestry projects has been how long it takes for income to be produced. For some projects, such as pine trees and mahogany, the bulk of the income is not received until after 20 years. Even for the shorter projects, such as blue gums, the main harvest proceeds are not produced until after 10 years. Fortunately, under new legislation, investors in forestry projects will be able to sell their investment after four years. This will lead to a secondary trading market, and mean that investors worried about being locked into the investment for too long will have an escape route if required.

For an investment to be worthwhile, it should produce a reasonable return before any tax advantages are taken into account. Some of the current projects have anticipated compounding returns of approximately 10 per cent, and in addition there are often incentives built in for the managers of the projects to produce better returns. This is done by allowing the project manager to share in any performance that exceeds the predicted return.

The problem of the managerial incompetence can also largely be avoided, due to the number of project managers operating today that have been in the industry for many years. Some managers have been operating successfully in the industry for long enough to have completed projects, on which investors have received a return on their investment.

An efficient manager can also be indicated by such things as ensuring value is added to products by controlling the processing of the raw material into the finished product. This is often demonstrated by the manager's continuing research and development into finding ways of improving the growing, harvesting and processing of the product.

Two other ways of deciding on the best project to invest in are price and the background of the manager. Some project managers started their involvement in the industry as growers and then developed the expertise to put together agribusiness investment projects themselves. Other investors come from a funds management background and either hire staff to do the growing or contract out the growing functions. The managers that come from a growing background tend to provide better value for money, as their projects often cost less then those promoted by the other managers. In addition, the grower managers have a closer association with the actual growing of the product and are more passionate about the industry, whereas managers who come from a funds management background often have a greater interest in the money side of the project ... and are as passionate about anything as bankers can ever be.

CHAPTER 11

Cars and tax

One area of tax legislation that affects more business owners than any other is the sections and regulations relating to motor vehicles. They are so complicated that, in most cases, the people in the automotive industry give incorrect advice about what is tax-deductible and what is not. And under self-assessment, if a taxpayer gets it wrong, it is the taxpayer and not the car salesperson that pays the penalties.

When you're considering purchasing a car, two main tax components should be taken into account: the depreciation cost limit, and the business use of the car. In 1980, the then federal government decided it wasn't fair for the tax system to subsidise the lifestyles of the rich and would-be famous. As a result, a depreciation cost limit was introduced that meant tax deductions were limited to vehicles up to a prescribed value.

Not all motor vehicles are caught by this limit: vehicles that are essentially commercial do not have the limit applied. However, vehicles that are primarily designed to carry private passengers — including vehicles designed to carry less than one tonne or fewer than nine passengers — are caught.

Originally, the cost limit was $18 000 and was meant to increase each year in line with inflation. This annual increase did occur until 1997, by which time the limit had risen to

$55 134, but since then it has only increased to $57 123 (for the 2006–07 tax year).

Applying depreciation cost limits to cars

The purchase of cars can affect not only income tax, but also the claiming of input tax credits under the GST system — the depreciation limit is used by the GST system to determine the input tax credit a business can claim when buying a motor vehicle.

Businesses can claim a credit for the business usage component of the GST paid on the purchase of a motor vehicle up to the depreciation cost limit. This means where the GST-inclusive cost of a car is below $57 123, a claim can be made for the business use of all of the GST in the price. For vehicles that exceed this limit, the input tax credit is limited to the business-use percentage of $5193.

So far, fairly plain sailing. However, the definition of the depreciation cost limit differs for income tax and GST. For GST purposes, the cost limit includes the GST charged, while for income tax the cost limit is after GST has been claimed. As a result, there are in effect two different limits: for the GST system the limit is $57 123 including GST, and for income tax purposes it's $62 709.

Let's look at an example of how this works. Say a car cost $61 000 and is used 100 per cent for business. If the owner is registered for GST, he or she could claim an input tax credit for the car up to the depreciation limit of $5193. Thus, the net cost of the car, after the input tax credit claim, is $55 807. As this is less than the depreciation cost limit of $57 123, it can be used for calculating the annual depreciation claim on the owner's income tax return.

Maximising car tax deductions

For many taxpayers, whether they are employed or operate a business, one of the biggest tax deductions will be for motor vehicles. There are five different ways to calculate and claim motor vehicle expenses:

- the kilometre method
- the 12 per cent of original value method
- the one-third of actual cost method
- the logbook method
- the fringe benefits tax method.

Note that the methods only apply to traditional passenger vehicles; different rules apply to more work-oriented vehicles. Vehicles designed to carry more than eight passengers, or a load of one tonne or more, can be claimed in full unless they are used for purely private purposes. Panel vans, taxis and utes of less than one tonne can also be claimed in full where the private use is limited to travel between a person's place of residence and place of business, or where private travel is minor, infrequent and irregular.

Like most things in life, the method requiring the greatest work—the logbook method—often produces the best tax result. To work out what the best method is for you, however, first make a rough estimate of what percentage business travel makes up of your total travel. 'Business travel' does not include driving from home to work and return, or any travel for private purposes. It does include driving from home to a business appointment then to work, driving from work to a business appointment then home, and any travel to carry out business from work.

When the vehicle is used to carry bulky tools or goods from home to work, this can also be classed as business travel. Examples of this are a retailer who stores goods at home and then transports them to the shop, a salesperson who must carry a wide range of samples at all times, and a carpenter who carries a compressor and other equipment in the back of a ute or station wagon.

Once the rough estimate of business and total kilometres has been arrived at, you will know approximately what percentage your business travel is. Where you estimate you will drive under 5000 business kilometres in a year, you must use the kilometre method unless you are prepared to keep a logbook for 12 weeks.

The kilometre method

Under the kilometre method, the tax deduction is arrived at by multiplying the business kilometres, up to a maximum of 5000 a year, by a cents per kilometre rate. No documentation needs to be kept to prove the number of kilometres claimed, but you must be able to show that you estimated the distance travelled in a reasonable way. For example, you might have looked at the number of business trips done in a month and the kilometres travelled for each trip, then multiplied the total for the month by 12.

The cents per kilometre rate varies depending on the engine size of the vehicle. The rates for the 2006–07 year were as shown in table 11.1, overleaf. (These rates apply to conventional cars only; for rotary cars and motorbikes different engine sizes and rates apply.)

Where two or more cars are owned in a year and used for business purposes, each of the cars can be claimed for using this method. The thing to remember is that you must be able to show you've used a reasonable method to estimate how much business travel is done in each car.

Here's an example. Let's say that an electrician owns a van set up with all of his equipment and tools, plus a ute and a car. The running costs of the van are claimed 100 per cent. He uses the ute sometimes when one of his employees is driving the van, and he uses his car when he visits customers to quote on a job. In this case, the electrician can use the kilometre method to claim a deduction for the ute and the car, based on his estimate of the business kilometres he drives in each of those vehicles.

Table 11.1: cents per kilometre (CPK) rates

Engine size	CPK rate
Up to 1600cc	58¢
1600cc to 2600cc	69¢
Over 2600cc	70¢

The 12 per cent of original cost method

Where a car does more than 5000 kilometres, any the other four methods can be used. With the 12 per cent of original cost method, the tax deduction is equal to the cost of the vehicle up to the depreciation cost limit of $57 123, multiplied by 12 per cent. The cost figure used in this calculation is the ex-GST cost of the car. For example, a car that cost $33 000 including GST would produce a tax deduction of $3600.

One-third of actual cost method

The one-third of total costs is calculated by dividing all running costs associated with the car by three. 'Running costs' include fuel, repairs, registration, insurance, motor association subscriptions, road and bridge tolls, lease payments, interest on loans and hire-purchase contracts, and depreciation. Table 11.2 shows at what point either the 12 per cent or one-third methods give a better tax deduction where a car does 5000 kilometres or more a year.

Table 11.2: comparison of 12 per cent
and one-third methods

Engine size	Deduction for 5000km	12 per cent method Best for cars costing more than:	One-third method Best when total costs are more than:
Up to1600cc	$2900	$24 167	$8700
1601cc to 2600cc	$3450	$28 750	$10 350
More than 2600cc	$3500	$29 167	$10 500

The logbook method

Under the logbook method, a record of your car travel must be kept for 12 weeks. Each logbook entry must show the day the journey began and ended, the odometer reading at the start and end of the journey, the length of the journey in kilometres and the reason for the journey.

In addition, the logbook as a whole must:

- show when the logbook period begins and ends
- give the odometer readings at the beginning and end of the logbook period
- give the total number of kilometres travelled during the logbook period
- list the number of kilometres travelled on business
- state the percentage that business kilometres made up of the total kilometres travelled.

At the end of the 12 weeks, the percentage of business use of the car is what you can claim of the total running costs of the car (including fuel, registration, insurance, repairs, lease, interest and depreciation, as before). Table 11.3 gives an example of how the logbook method works, using a business-use figure of 70 per cent.

Table 11.3: calculating the deduction

Car expenses for year	$
Petrol	3600
Repairs	800
Registration	600
Insurance	750
Interest on chattel mortgage	2800
Depreciation	7400
Total costs	**15950**
Tax deduction for 70 per cent business use	**11165**

The tax regulations do not require you to record all of your travel in a logbook — only the business travel. However, this can be a trap, as when you don't have to record all travel you often miss some business travel. It's far safer to record everything.

To make the job of keeping a logbook easier, you should systemise the process and have it become a routine. Here's a good system to follow: every time you get in the car, write in the date of the journey, the starting odometer reading and the purpose of the trip. This will give you all the information needed, as the odometer reading at the start of your next trip is automatically the closing reading for the previous trip. Once the 12 weeks are up, or at periodic intervals, the rest of the information can be completed and the distance of each journey calculated.

To make the job easier, you can also use abbreviations or codes for your regular trips. For example, 'CV' for 'customer visit' and 'PM' for 'picking up materials'. Then, after writing the date and starting kilometre reading in the logbook, you only have to write 'CV' or 'PM' and the suburb driven to.

Another way of maximising your percentage of business travel is to put some thought into each trip. For example, instead of travelling from home to your business and then on to see a client, you should go to the client first. Then, all of the travel from home to business will be tax-deductible.

In addition, when you use your car for business combine it with a private trip. For example, if you have to do a trip to the bank or post office, get your lunch or do some other private shopping at the same time. This strategy only works, however, as long as the private travel is incidental to the business travel. It would not be acceptable, say, to class a trip that involved a detour of more than a kilometre for a private purpose as all business related.

Once the logbook has been kept for the 12 weeks, that logbook lasts for 5 years. In addition to the logbook, a record must be kept at the end of each tax year that shows the starting and closing odometer reading for the year, and records the car's make, model, registration number and engine capacity.

If the car is sold and a new car bought, you do not have to do a new logbook if the business use of the new car will be the same as the old car. In this situation, a formal nomination must be made in writing that specifies the replacement date, and each car should be clearly identified. This nomination should be retained in case the ATO requests to see it.

The fringe benefits tax method

The final way to claim tax deductions for cars is using the FBT provisions of the tax act. To do this, you must be employed by your business: the FBT method is not available to someone who is self-employed. The method works best where:

- the car is used for business purposes very little
- tax is payable by the individual at 46.5 per cent
- the car costs less than $57 123 and is subject to finance
- the car does more than 25 000 kilometres a year.

For a fuller explanation of the FBT method, see page 100.

Financing cars effectively

Purchasing motor vehicles can be a confusing experience. Many decisions must be made, such as whose name the vehicle should be purchased in, how much of the purchase cost should be financed and what sort of finance is best for the purposes of income tax (see chapter 8 for the impact of car purchases on GST). The answer to these questions depends largely on whether the car is being purchased for business or private purposes.

In general terms, it does not make a great deal of difference whether a car is purchased in an individual's name or a business name. It is important, however, to make sure that the financing of the car is done correctly. A wrong decision can have adverse consequences for both income tax and GST.

When a car is to be used for predominantly private purposes, the amount being financed should be kept to a minimum. For a car that will have a high proportion of business use, by contrast, the financing should be maximised. The trade-in on the car being replaced should be used to repay any private debt, such as a home loan, and the full cost of the new vehicle financed.

The most common forms of finance that can be used to purchase a car are:

- leases
- hire-purchase (HP) contracts
- chattel mortgage (CM) contracts
- personal loans
- by increasing a home loan.

Personal loans should only be used as a last resort, as they tend to have a much higher interest rate than the other financing options, and only small amounts can be borrowed.

Increasing a home loan through a redraw facility or a line of credit can be effective where the car being financed is to be used for private purposes. If the car will be used for business purposes, however, there can be problems. When a loan is made up of both business and private borrowings, repayments of principal are applied equally to the tax-deductible and non-tax-deductible portions of the loan. This is not tax-efficient. It is better to have two separate loans, so that the principal repayments on the private loan can be maximised while the repayments on the tax-deductible loan are minimised.

Despite popular opinion, there is not a great deal of difference between the after-tax cost of financing a car using a lease, HP or CM. Over a five-year period, a car worth approximately $30 000 will cost $94 more after tax using a lease rather than the other two methods. There are, however, other important considerations that should be taken into account.

A HP or CM contract should be used if you cannot be sure that the car will be kept for the whole period of the finance contract. This is because the payout value of a lease is calculated differently than the others, and as a result, where a leased car is sold before the end of the contract the payout value can be higher than if the car had been financed using a HP or CM contract.

If you are sure that you will keep the car for the full term of the finance contract a lease can be better, despite costing slightly more—because it takes a lot more work to calculate the tax deduction for a HP or CM contract than a lease. The tax-deductible amount for a lease is simply the business-use component of the lease payments. Whereas, under HP or CM contracts, a claim must be made for both the business use portion of the contract's interest cost and the depreciation of the car up to the depreciation cost limit. The only advantage that HP or CM contracts have over leases is that the tax deductions can be greater in the first few years, due to the depreciation claim (although over the full term of the contact, the after-tax cost is almost the same).

If you are not worried about the extra work and want to use a HP or CM contract, be aware that there can be a major GST difference between the two depending on how you account for GST. Under the accrual method (detailed in chapter 8), the GST included in the cost of the car can be used as a credit in the BAS period it is purchased. However, under the cash method of accounting for GST, using a HP contract means the GST credit cannot be claimed as a lump sum, but must be claimed proportionally over the life of the contract. Whereas if a CM contract is used instead, the full amount of GST can still be claimed in the period the car was purchased.

Let's look at an example of the difference between the two forms of finance. Say a car is purchased in September 2008 for $52 800. The GST included in the cost would be $4800. Under the cash method of accounting, a HP contract taken out for 48 months would produce a GST input tax credit of $100 in the first quarter and then $300 a quarter until the last quarter, when $200 could be claimed. Using a CM contract a claim of $4800 could be made for the September 2008 quarter.

For a lease, by the way, the finance company gets the benefit of the GST credit, which is then passed on in the form of a lower amount financed. For example, if a car costs $31 250, the HP and CM contracts will be for the full amount, while under a lease the amount financed will be $28 409. Of course, if you are using the accrual method of accounting and chose a HP or CM contract, you could claim the GST of $2841 as a credit in the period the car was purchased, as well.

Clearly, the question of which is the best way to finance a car is not simple. There are many factors to consider. The important lesson is to not take advice from the car salesperson or finance officer, but to ask for advice from your accountant. He or she can also advise you if the interest charge seems too high and possibly recommend another finance provider.

CHAPTER 12

Minimising tax on selling a business

In recent years, successive federal governments have recognised the important part that small business plays in the Australian economy. In addition, it was recognised that the capital gains tax laws as originally drafted would unfairly burden small business owners. It is common for small business owners to work extremely long hours, sometimes for less money than their employees, and often with the reward coming only when they sell the business. As a result, various concessions have been introduced that directly benefit small business owners, and these will be discussed later in the chapter.

To qualify for this CGT relief, several tests must be passed. The first requires that the taxpayer wanting to claim the concessions is a SBE, or a partner in a partnership that is an SBE (for a detailed explanation of the SBE system, refer to chapter 4). The other tests are:

- the net assets test
- the active assets test
- the significant individual test for companies and trusts.

Net assets test

To pass the net assets test, the net assets of the taxpayer—including the net assets of connected entities, affiliates and entities connected with affiliates—must be less than $6 million. This test was designed to ensure people and entities could not access the CGT concessions by having multiple entities, or having assets owned by other people they can control.

Net assets for individual owners

The calculation of net assets is a lot simpler when individuals own the business. In this case, the net asset value is calculated by subtracting the total value of their liabilities, such as investment loans and overdrafts, from the total value of their investment and business assets, such as shares and rental properties.

For individuals, some assets must not be included in the net asset value. These include the value of:

- personal and private-use assets, such as homes or holiday houses
- a dwelling that produces assessable rental income, where a loan was used to purchase the property but a tax deduction cannot be claimed for any interest on this loan
- a pension, annuity or allowance paid by a super fund
- amounts held in a superannuation fund still in the accumulation phase
- life insurance policies.

Net assets for businesses

For any business, the net value is calculated by deducting total liabilities of the entity, such as hire-purchase contracts and provisions made for holiday pay and long service leave, from the market value of the entity's assets. The 'market value' is not the cost of the assets but what they could be sold for.

If you don't go to the trouble of having the market value of your business's various assets assessed, you could find too late that it fails the net asset value test and is denied access to the small business CGT concessions. If market values are obtained and a problem is discovered later, steps can be taken to help pass the test. One strategy would be to transfer a business property into a super fund.

The important thing to remember is that the net asset value includes the net assets of a taxpayer's affiliates and connected entities, as well as the taxpayer individually.

Connected and affiliated entities

A 'connected entity' is one that is controlled by another entity, or two or more entities that are controlled by another entity. There are various tests to determine whether one entity controls another and is therefore 'connected'. For all entities except discretionary trusts, an entity will be connected to another entity if it owns enough of the second entity's units or shares to entitle it to at least 40 per cent of the capital or net income distributions. A company can also be a connected entity if another entity or person owns at least 40 per cent of the voting rights in the company.

A discretionary trust is a connected entity if another entity or person can reasonably be expected to exercise control over the trustee of the trust. In addition, any entity or individual that receives at least 40 per cent of the income or capital distributions from the trust in a year is regarded as connected.

'Affiliates' can only be companies or individuals. An entity is considered an affiliate if it can reasonably be expected to act in accordance with the wishes and directions of the other company or individual. This can mean, in some circumstances, that the assets of a spouse can be included in the net assets test. However, for this to happen there would need to be a business connection between the couple; where there is no connection the spouse's assets are not necessarily included.

Here's an example of how this works. Sandy owns a clothing store, and her husband Danny works with her in the business. Although she has no other assets, Danny owns a half-share of a commercial building worth $12 million. Let's say Sandy sells the business and receives $200 000 for the goodwill. There is a high likelihood that Danny would be regarded as an affiliate, and Sandy would not be eligible to receive the CGT concessions.

If Danny ran a building business and was not involved in the running of Sandy's business, there's a greater chance that he would not be classed as an affiliate, and that his assets would not be included for the net assets test.

The sections of the tax act dealing with connected and affiliate entities are extremely complicated. If you are worried about having entities or individuals caught by these provisions, professional advice should be sought.

Active assets tests

There are two tests used to decide what is an active asset. First, an active asset must have been used in the carrying on of the business (a factory or office, for example), or must be an intangible asset connected with the business (such as goodwill or trademarks). Active assets can also include shares in a company if 80 per cent of the value of the company is made up of active assets. They also include assets owned by any other entities connected with the business.

This last inclusion means that a business can be operated through a company or trust, and other business assets such as premises can be owned by an individual or other entities connected with a taxpayer. In this case, the other business assets are also eligible for the CGT concessions, even when the business rents the assets from their owners.

For example, say Stan and Oliver are dentists and run their dental practice through a company. They also own the surgery used by the practice, in partnership as individuals. In 2008 they decide to transfer the surgery into their self-managed super fund and make a capital gain of $1 million. They pass the net assets test, and as the surgery is an active asset and they are connected with the dental practice, they can use the retirement exemption so that no tax is paid on the capital gain.

The second test is that the asset must have been an active asset for a set period during the time it was owned. This test was included to stop taxpayers changing the use of an asset just to get the CGT concessions. Assets owned for less than 15 years must have been active assets for at least half of the time; assets owned for more than 15 years must have been active assets for at least seven and a half years.

Here's an example. Olivia owns a factory. If she had owned the factory for 10 years, rented it to a tenant for seven of those years and used it as business premises for three years, it would not be classed as an active asset. If, on the other hand, she'd used it as business premises for six years and rented it for four years, it would be classed as an active asset. If she'd owned the factory for 20 years, and used it to run her business from for eight years, it would be classed as an active asset.

Significant individual test

Businesses operated through a company or a trust must pass one further test. Unlike partnerships, where all of the partners can receive the small business CGT concessions, for companies and trusts these concessions are limited to people who pass the significant individual test.

In a company, a person qualifies as a significant individual by having at least 20 per cent of the voting shares in the company, and being entitled to receive at least 20 per cent of the company's income and capital. Thus, if there are five shareholders in a company, each with 20 per cent of the shares they can all get the CGT small business concessions. The concessions also pass to the spouses of significant individuals, where the spouses have an ownership in the company of more than zero.

There is a similar test for fixed and unit trusts. People are classed as significant individuals if they own enough units to entitle them to at least 20 per cent of the income and capital distributions from the trust. For discretionary trusts, a person passes this test if he or she receives at least 20 per cent of the income and capital distributed in the year the capital gain is made.

The four concessions

Once the various tests have been passed, a taxpayer can get access to the four concessions on offer. They are:

- the 15-year asset exemption
- the 50 per cent reduction for active assets
- the retirement exemption
- the rollover deferral concession.

These concessions are available after the 50 per cent general capital gains tax exemption has been claimed. Under the 15-year asset exemption, the whole of the capital gain is exempt from tax if several conditions are met. For the other three concessions, capital losses must be offset against the capital gain before the concessions are applied.

The 15-year asset exemption

To be eligible for the 15-year asset exemption, in addition to meeting the other small business conditions, the entity must have continuously owned the asset for the 15-year period leading up to the time it is sold.

Where the entity owning the business is a company or trust, there must have been a significant individual for the full 15 years. For companies and fixed trusts, this is relatively easy. For a discretionary trust, where distributions of income can change between individuals on a year-to-year basis, one person must have received at least 20 per cent of the distributions for this test to be met.

Once the 15-year period requirement has been met, the exemption can be claimed if the individual owning the business, or the significant individual from the company or trust, retires or becomes permanently incapacitated. For shareholders, unitholders, and beneficiaries, any payment made by the company or trust within two years of the sale of the asset is also exempt.

Once the conditions are met, the 15-year asset exemption means none of the capital gain is taxable, and is not reduced by any capital losses. Apart from the $6 million net assets limit, there is no limit on the amount of capital gain that will qualify for this concession. Where a company or trust operates the business, any payment resulting from the capital gain for a period of two years after the gain occurred will be exempt for the significant individual.

The 50 per cent active assets discount

Where all of the relevant tests have been passed, a capital gain made on an active asset can be discounted by 50 per cent. This discount can be used after the general 50 per cent discount available to individuals and trusts has been used—meaning that when this discount is claimed in conjunction with the general discount, effectively only 25 per cent of the capital gain is taxable.

The exemption is, however, only of major benefit for individuals. Where a fixed trust (such as a unit trust) or a company owns a business, it effectively does not get the benefit of the 50 per cent active asset exemption. This is because when a company makes a capital gain and claims the 50 per cent active asset exemption, it results in a non-taxable profit being made. If this profit is distributed to shareholders, it is treated as an unfranked dividend, and tax is paid on the previously exempted amount.

A similar situation happens with a unit trust. If a trust claims the 50 per cent active asset exemption and then distributes the non-taxable amount to its unitholders, that amount must be used to decrease the original purchase cost of the units. This results in more capital gains tax being paid when the units are sold or the trust is wound up.

One of the only ways that companies and fixed trusts can reduce this adverse tax effect is to not distribute the amount claimed for the active asset exemption. If the funds are retained until the company or trust is wound up, and distributed as capital proceeds then, the exempt gain then receives the 50 per cent general capital gains discount.

When a business is owned by a discretionary trust, it is the individual beneficiaries who receive the 50 per cent active asset exemption on the capital gain distributed — so the full benefit of the exemption is received.

The retirement exemption

Under the retirement exemption, an individual can escape paying CGT on a gain up to a lifetime limit of $500 000. As this exemption can be applied after the 50 per cent general discount and the 50 per cent active assets discount, a capital gain of up to $2 million can be made by an individual with no tax being paid.

The retirement exemption does however require the capital proceeds from the sale of a business to be used in connection with retirement. People who are 55 or over can receive the funds directly and use them as they want. People under 55 must meet more stringent conditions to obtain the retirement benefit: the sale proceeds eligible for the retirement exemption must be rolled over into a super fund, with the funds being paid directly by the business into the super fund. The proceeds cannot be paid via the individual into the super fund.

The amount of the retirement exemption must also be paid within the later of seven days of the proceeds of the sale being received or seven days of choosing to use this exemption. As the choice is made on the tax return of the individual or the entity owning the business, this second deadline is effectively within seven days of the tax return being lodged.

Where the sale proceeds for a business are received in the year it is sold, the later of the two dates will be the tax return lodgement date. This is because the cash is received in one tax year but the election is made in the following year. A business sold with vendor's finance over a number of years will mean the later of the two dates will be when the proceeds are received. Sale proceeds received in instalments require that a portion of each amount received, equal to the percentage that the retirement exemption is of the total sale proceeds, be rolled over into a super fund within seven days of each instalment being received.

The rollover deferral concession

The final CGT small business benefit is called 'rollover relief'. Under this concession, the capital gain rolled over decreases the cost of a replacement active asset purchased, such as goodwill or plant and equipment. The rollover occurs when funds are used to purchase a replacement asset or improve an existing asset.

For example, say that Burt sells his accounting business in September 2007 and, after claiming the various exemptions, is left with a capital gain of $350 000. He decides to go into business as a financial planner in March 2008. He uses $350 000 from the proceeds of the sale of his previous business to build an office costing $450 000 on land purchased by him in 2004. As such, the office qualifies as an improvement, and he can claim the rollover concession for the $350 000 spent.

To receive the rollover relief, the replacement asset or improvement must be an active asset. This not only includes business assets such as plant, machinery or business premises, but also shares in a company or units in a unit trust that owns an active asset such as a business. Where the rollover concession is claimed for ownership of a company or a trust, the person making the claim must end up with a controlling percentage of the entity.

The replacement asset can be purchased, or the improvement made, up to one year before or two years after the date of the capital gains tax event in question. A replacement asset or improvement will also qualify if it is bought or made within 12 months of receiving an increased payout from the sale. An increased payout can happen when a business is sold subject to achieving certain performance benchmarks, such as sales volume, and the payment is made after the two years have elapsed.

The replacement asset rollover concession affects the potential future capital gain of the replacement asset, but does not decrease the cost base for depreciation purposes. As a result, in most cases tax is not saved — it is only postponed until the replacement asset is sold.

Nevertheless, by delaying the capital gain, in some circumstances an actual tax saving can be achieved. This occurs when tax rates are decreased (such as when the two top tax rates dropped down to 40 per cent and 45 per cent), and when tax thresholds change (such as will happen in the 2009 financial year, when the top tax threshold increases from $150 000 to $180 000).

The best way to illustrate how all of the CGT small business concessions work is with the following example. William, a 50-year-old computer software developer, sold his computer software business on 1 April 2008 for $4 million, and made a $3 million capital gain.

Bill owns a house worth $1 million, has a holiday house worth $600 000 and has $950 000 in superannuation. In addition to his business, he has a rental property with a market value of $600 000 (at the time of selling his business), and an investment loan on that property of $300 000. So, the assets classed in the net assets test add up to $4 300 000. As such, he has no more than $6 million in net assets and therefore meets the net asset test for small business CGT relief.

The $3 million capital gain related to the business's trademarks and copyright, its client database, and a value for goodwill. Therefore, the gain has been made on only active assets, and the full gain qualifies for the CGT concessions.

The first concession he claims is the general 50 per cent concession open to individuals and most trusts. The next concessions claimed are the 50 per cent active asset exemption and the retirement exemption. Being under 55, Bill rolls the maximum retirement exemption of $500 000 into a super fund. After these three concessions he is left with an assessable capital gain of $250 000.

In the 2008 tax year, he has already earned assessable income of $100 000. If he does nothing further, income tax of $110 000 will be paid on the residual assessable capital gain of $250 000. However, after a year off, Bill decides to buy a franchise business costing $1 million. As this business is purchased within two years of making the capital gain, he claims the rollover relief exemption and pays no tax on the $250 000 for the 2008 financial year.

Bill works in the franchise business for two years, but gets sick of the long hours and sells it for $1 100 000 in the 2010 year. He now pays tax on the $250 000 rolled over. He claims the general exemption and the active asset exemption on the $100 000 capital gain made on the sale of the franchise business, resulting in him paying tax on a residual capital gain of $25 000. Table 12.1 sets out this whole situation.

Table 12.1: Bill's CGT concessions

Bill's private assets, not counted in net assets test	$
Home	1 000 000
Holiday house	600 000
Superannuation	950 000
	2 550 000
Bill's assets counted in the net assets test	**$**
Proceeds from sale of business	4 000 000
Rental property	600 000
	4 600 000
Less investment loan	300 000
Total value of net assets	**4 300 000**
	$
Capital gain made on sale of business	3 000 000
Less 50 per cent general discount	1 500 000
Less 50 per cent active asset discount	750 000
Less amount rolled into super under retirement exemption	500 000
Assessable capital gain	**250 000**
Rollover exemption used to help with purchase of franchise	250 000
Capital gain made on sale of franchise	100 000
Less 50 per cent general discount	50 000
Less 50 per cent active asset discount	25 000
Residual capital gain	**25 000**

Due to the complicated nature of the various laws, and the way in which the small business CGT concessions can be used, professional advice should be obtained whenever a capital gain is made.

CHAPTER 13

Surviving a tax audit

The federal and state governments recognise how much extra tax revenue is produced from increased compliance activities. Over recent federal budgets, the states and territories have even agreed to forego a portion of their GST revenue so that more money can be allocated to the ATO for compliance activities.

The higher the tax-risk industry you operate in, the greater the likelihood that you will be audited or reviewed. For example, if you operate in an industry where large amounts of cash are received, such as with takeaway food shops and building contractors, you have a higher chance of being audited.

Taxpayers can be selected for an audit for many reasons. It can be because they were reported to the ATO for suspected tax evasion, or it can result from the financial information they lodge ringing alarm bells in the ATO. During the 2003–2004 audit program, almost 34 000 businesses received 'please explain' letters because their financial performance did not match that of their industry.

Another area where the information provided can lead to compliance activity is BAS returns. If you have a large GST refund from purchasing costly plant and equipment, or your poor trading results mean that GST refunds are claimed over succeeding quarters, there is a high chance your business will be selected for compliance checks.

What many business owners and taxpayers forget is that under the self-assessment tax system the ATO initially accepts all tax returns lodged. A common complaint of many taxpayers, when their accountant tells them something is not tax-deductible, is that it must be deductible because they know other people who are successfully claiming it. In these cases the claim has not been allowed, it just hasn't been checked.

What to do if you are selected for an audit

Once you become aware that you have been selected for an audit, you should let your accountant know as soon as possible. They can deal with the ATO on your behalf and advise you of what the audit involves and what records need to be produced. They can also conduct a preliminary review to check if there are any areas that could be of concern to the ATO.

The next thing to do is to cooperate with the ATO as much as possible. Unfortunately, some people take a combative approach when they are selected for an audit. Doing this achieves nothing except putting the auditor in the sort of frame of mind that leads to penalties being imposed at the maximum rate.

On the other hand, if all possible assistance is provided to the auditor there is a greater likelihood that if he or she has discretion about penalties, the penalties will be reduced. On numerous occasions when I have helped clients though an ATO audit, a better result has always been achieved by being cooperative.

One client I assisted with an employer obligation audit had not paid super on wages paid as a piece rate. This resulted in them having a sizable SGC liability. However, because they cooperated fully with the ATO auditors, they were able to self-assess their own SGC debt and pay the required amount. The tax office could instead have raised an SGC liability notice, and imposed penalties of up to 200 per cent of the superannuation shortfall.

The ATO has made it clear it prefers to regard its activities as 'compliance improvement audits'. But if tax officers find an employer has deliberately not done the right thing, or is being uncooperative, they can soon shift into compliance enforcement mode and impose maximum penalties.

Penalties and fines

Under the income tax act, the ATO has the ability to impose penalties when taxpayers make mistakes. And since the GST honeymoon period finished, any returns found to be incorrect — including BAS forms — have penalties imposed strictly in accordance with ATO guidelines.

When the ATO discovers tax or GST has been underpaid, either by way of a voluntary disclosure or because of an audit, two penalties can be imposed. The first is not tax-deductible, and is imposed for having made a false or misleading statement. The second penalty is in the form of an interest charge, and is tax-deductible. This second penalty is called a 'general interest charge' (GIC) and is designed to compensate the ATO for having received tax revenue late.

General interest charges

Say a business made a mistake on a BAS that resulted in an underpayment of GST of $10000, and the error was discovered 12 months after the GST should have been paid. A GIC penalty of approximately $1250 would be imposed. In this situation, where the ATO did not receive the GST when it should have and the business had the use of that GST for 12 months, it is not unfair that the interest penalty is imposed.

What is unfair is when the ATO imposes penalties despite the fact that all revenue that should have been collected was received on time. This injustice is made even worse when a GIC is imposed on businesses that make an innocent mistake by tax auditors strictly enforcing the smallest requirements of the tax and GST legislation.

With the increased focus by the ATO on conducting GST, employer obligation, and income tax audits, many more taxpayers are likely to have errors discovered by the ATO. When this happens, they are likely to be required to pay GIC penalties, even though in some cases the ATO has not really been disadvantaged.

When a business claims an input tax credit for GST paid, it must be in possession of a valid tax invoice from the supplier of the good or service. Amongst other information, tax invoice must have the name and ABN of the supplier.

Under the GST legislation there is a provision for a business to raise invoices on behalf of suppliers: these are called 'recipient-created tax invoices'. Say, for example, a business has a contractor working for it on a regular basis. It prepares an invoice for work done by the contractor for $11000 including GST. The supplier (the contractor) sends off the $1000 of GST it has collected, and the business that issued the invoice claims a credit for the $1000 in GST it paid. The net effect in GST terms for the ATO is zero.

This fact is not always given due weight by the ATO, however. One business subjected to a GST audit found that, due to a computer glitch, all of the recipient-created invoices it had issued had been printed without suppliers' ABNs. All of the relevant details were in the computer files, but the paper tax invoice were missing that one detail. The ATO, in its wisdom, issued 36 amended BAS returns, raising a GST debt of $3.7 million for the offending business. After the business had printed tax invoices showing the missing ABN information, it was immediately able to make another claim for the $3.7 million in GST input tax.

In this case, the suppliers had sent the GST collected to the ATO and, although the recipient-created tax invoices were not technically correct, the business audited had paid GST and was entitled to claim it. In what can only be described as a mean-spirited act, the ATO nevertheless charged that business with a GIC penalty of $1.1 million.

Another compliance program conducted by the ATO relates to the non-commercial loss provisions. Where mistakes are made, with incorrect claims for business losses having been made, the ATO can impose penalties for having made a false or misleading statement.

Penalties for false or misleading statements

Before it imposes a penalty for having made a false or misleading statement, the ATO first establishes whether the taxpayer or their agent took reasonable care. Only where the tax office believes reasonable care was not taken will the penalty for having made a false or misleading statement be imposed.

Taxpayers who have made a genuine attempt to follow the relevant tax laws, but make an honest mistake, would be regarded as taking reasonable care and no penalty would be imposed. Examples of reasonable care not being taken are where a taxpayer does not have the required documentary evidence to support a tax deduction, income is omitted from a return, or the taxpayer does not follow a recommendation of their agent on a matter of compliance.

The maximum penalty for making a false or misleading statement is $2200 for a first offence and $4400 for a subsequent offence. In most cases, these penalties are not applied at the maximum rate. For example, the maximum penalty for the late lodgment of tax and other returns is also $2200, but the recommended penalty for a first offence is between $200 and $500.

Anyone who has incorrectly claimed a tax deduction, or offset non-commercial losses against other income, would be well advised to let the ATO know of the mistake, instead of letting the error be discovered during an audit. Taxpayers who voluntarily disclose an error will not have a penalty imposed if the tax shortfall is less than $1000; if the shortfall amount is more than $1000, the penalty will be discounted by 80 per cent.

Employer obligation audits

One area where the ATO has increased its audit activities is related to employer obligations including PAYG withholding, superannuation guarantee, eligible termination payments and fringe benefits tax. Using its computer data-matching facilities, the ATO compares the information shown on a business's quarterly BAS statements, annual PAYG summary and tax return. Where discrepancies occur, the employer can become a candidate for an audit.

Employers are first advised that they've been selected for an audit by phone. Either the business or their tax agent is contacted, and a mutually convenient time arranged for all relevant records and documents to be inspected. The audit can also take place at a location convenient for the business—perhaps at the premises of the accountant.

A letter is then sent by the ATO detailing all of the records required to be produced. These can include payroll records, PAYG annual summaries for all employees, and super guarantee records, including dates of payment.

The cost of having resources taken up with an audit, combined with the potential financial penalties of not keeping the correct records or not paying contributions on time, should be enough incentive to ensure all employers meet their obligations.

Penalties relating to superannuation guarantee contributions

Be aware in particular that, due to the incredibly harsh way that the SGC legislation is written, very little discretion is given to the ATO on errors in this area—even when innocent mistakes are made. The SG commitments must be paid quarterly, and if employers don't pay enough super or miss the deadline for payment, the penalties imposed are both punitive and inflexible.

Tax for Small Business

All employees who earn more than $450 a month, with very few exceptions, must have SG contributions of 9 per cent made on their behalf. Employees excluded include:

- those over 70
- those under 18 and working less than 30 hours a week
- anyone doing private or domestic work for less than 30 hours a week
- those who have elected not to receive superannuation because they have exceeded their pension reasonable benefit limit.

The SG cannot be avoided by classing an employee as a contractor, even if they have their own ABN. Where contractors wholly or principally supply their labour to the employer (in other words, where more than half of the contract value is for the supply of labour) they will be classed as employees for SG purposes. If two or more individuals contract through a partnership, however, the SG obligations do not apply.

Where a short payment occurs because of a clerical error or an incorrect interpretation of what super must be paid on, wages not previously counted for superannuation must then be included. In addition to the SG penalty being payable, an interest penalty is also payable on the underpayments of super, backdated to the start of the period in question. For a quarterly commitment, the penalty is calculated back to the start of the quarter.

The deadlines for payment of superannuation are the 28th day following the end of each quarter. There is absolutely no latitude with regard to these deadlines. Some employers can get confused with their December quarter deadline, but even though the BAS for that quarter does not need to be lodged and paid until 28 February, the SG contributions must still be made by January 28.

If these quarterly deadlines are missed by even one day, an employer becomes liable for the SG charge, which is not tax-deductible. An SG charge statement must be completed and lodged with the ATO by the 28th day of the month following the day the original SG contributions should have been made.

If the SG error is found within the second period, the SG charge can be paid direct to a super fund. If this deadline is missed, the payment and SG charge statement must be sent directly to the ATO. When this occurs, employers must also pay an interest penalty and an administration fee.

If you are advised that you have been selected for an employer tax obligation audit, you should review all the areas that will be checked to make sure you have met all of your obligations. If you discover you have underpaid SG, paid it late, or not paid it all, the situation cannot be fixed by simply paying the required amount to a super fund.

Penalties relating to fringe benefits

If the complex SG regulations weren't enough, the intricacies of the fringe benefits legislation create another major problem area covered by an employer obligations audit.

The major focus of the FBT part of an audit is on the employer having all of the required documentation—car logbooks, car kilometre records, employee declarations, entertainment records, and so on. Employers must not rely on assurances from employees that they have the logbooks or other required records.

Where any of these records cannot be produced, the tax office is required to charge FBT in the most efficient manner. When it comes to car fringe benefits this will mean that, in the absence of a logbook that supports the business usage of a vehicle, the statutory method will be used. Under this method the FBT payable is based on the cost of the car and the number of kilometres driven each year.

Tax audit insurance

Businesses can take out compliance audit insurance to help pay the costs associated with an audit. The insurance policies tend to cover not only tax audits but also other compliance audits, such as those conducted by the WorkCover authorities.

The insurance does not provide money to pay any penalties imposed, but it does provide funding towards the fees of the professionals who assist you with the audit. This includes the fees charged by the accountant who deals with the ATO on your behalf and helps with the audit process.

Some policies will also provide funds to pay any overtime worked by employees in order to prepare for or be present at the audit. Policies can also provide cover for the travelling and accommodation expenses incurred by you and any of your employees who are required to attend the audit.

The cost of the insurance premium can differ according to the amount of cover required, and sometimes according to the size and turnover of the business as well. Premiums will also differ between insurance companies. In most cases, audit insurance is provided through accountants instead of being available to a business directly.

Given the increasing likelihood of receiving an audit at some time, even if your business has done nothing wrong, it makes sense to contact your accountant and ask if he or she offers audit insurance. It could be well worth the investment—even a simple audit can cost a business over $1000 in accounting fees.

CHAPTER 14

Getting the right advice

The task of running a small business gets harder every year. Not only do owners have to try and grow their business, they also have to cope with an increasing number of tax laws and other regulations. In addition to income tax, they have to deal with GST, superannuation guarantee, FBT and WorkCover issues on a regular basis.

The introduction of the new tax system in 2000 also meant an increase in workloads for many people. Business owners, in a lot of cases, were forced to either work extra hours on administrative tasks or employ someone else to do the work, and some owners regard this extra bookkeeping as a major imposition, believing that they know how their business is going just from working in it.

However, this belief has been proven false time and again. I've spent over 30 years as a public accountant working with small businesses, and two things come to my mind. The first is that a number of businesses fail, and despite all of the other reasons given for these failures, the common factor has been a lack of adequate financial records and management systems.

The second thing is that many businesses need to borrow money. And, if a business owner wants to borrow from a bank at a reasonable interest rate, he or she needs to prepare regular financial statements. There should also be an annual cash flow budget that demonstrates what the loan is needed for and how it can be repaid.

Tax compliance and improving a business

There's a lesson here that can be learned from the sporting arena. When people aren't serious about their sport, they tend to just do it. However, if they want to be the best they can, whether as a professional or as a dedicated amateur, they need to measure constantly how they are performing. A tennis player will measure such things as unforced errors, faults, aces and winning volleys. A footballer will measure number of possessions, effective kicks and handballs, marks and tackles. The same principle applies to business owners: the administration that is required by law is actually a tool they can use to manage their business better.

Of course, the act of measuring by itself does not guarantee success: it's what is done with the information that is important. Tennis players who know they are serving too many faults can start to work on improving their service action, for example. In most sports, significantly, players don't try and do this by themselves. The footballer has the help of the team coach or a specialist coach. The golfer can get help from a golf professional.

A business owner can also seek help in navigating their way through the various regulations, and improving their business. If you belong to a trade association or a professional body, this can be a source of assistance, for example. However, a primary source of assistance for business owners should be their accountant. Accountants' training and experience makes them well suited to assisting with compliance matters, and acting as coach and mentor to help grow the business. The sad fact is, however, they are often only used to lodge tax returns.

The cost/benefit of using an accountant

One reason accountants are not consulted more is that they are sometimes regarded as a necessary evil to help keep the taxman at bay. Business owners with this mindset tend to concentrate more on the cost of things, instead of weighing up business decisions in terms of cost and benefit.

These owners tend to make decisions by themselves rather than phoning for advice. This can be a false economy, as the benefit gained from the advice will often outweigh the cost. One example of this is a business owner who didn't telephone their accountant when buying a new vehicle, simply because the phone call would cost between $50 and $80. The business used the cash method of accounting for GST reporting. Because they financed the car with a hire-purchase contract, their GST claim was limited to $500 a quarter over a three-year term. If they had asked for advice they would have been told to use a chattel mortgage, resulting in a GST claim of $3000 in the quarter the car was purchased, and thus significant cash flow advantages.

Most accountants charge for their services on a time basis. This means the size of the fee depends on the time taken to do the job and the hourly rate of the person doing the work. The hourly rate charged will differ within an accounting practice depending on who is doing the work, and will differ between accounting practices.

Within accounting firms, the hourly rate charged depends on the level of qualification and the years of experience of the person doing the work. For example, an accountant with five years of experience might have a charge rate of $110 an hour; a capital gains specialist with over 20 years of experience might have a charge rate of $300 an hour.

Fee levels between accounting firms will differ depending on the location of the practice. For example, an accounting firm with beautiful offices in the city will in most cases charge its staff out at higher rates than a firm operating from a modest office in the outer suburbs. If the accountant has the right experience, the level of service is often the same and the only difference is the fee charged.

Once you recognise that the longer an accounting job takes the more it costs, you can save on fees by providing all of the information required to do the job. This means you supply not only the financial information, but copies of supporting documentation such as bank statements, loan statements and completed BAS forms. The more information your accountant has to chase you for, the more the fee will be.

Poor service from an accountant

Another, more serious, reason that some business owners do not contact their accountant more often is the poor level of professional service they receive. Business owners want to be able to get advice when they need it, not when their accountant feels like taking their calls.

The most common complaints about accountants are:

- They are always hard to contact and their calls are screened.
- They never return phone calls.
- They do not complete work on time, so late lodgment penalties are imposed by the ATO that the client is made to pay.
- They are not able to answer basic questions like, 'Why am I paying so much tax?'

- They are not proactive and do not recommend ways to improve the business or save tax.
- They don't take responsibility for mistakes they make.

Accountant or tax agent?

If you are interested in making as much money as possible, and paying as little tax as you have to, you need to work out if you have an accountant or a tax agent. A tax agent is only interested in preparing and lodging tax returns and the other forms and statements required by the ATO. He or she tends to only look backwards and is not interested in offering advice.

An accountant, however, not only prepares and lodges the forms but also provides advice on ways to help improve the financial wellbeing of the business and its owners. This help and advice is often proactive, and will result in tax being paid at the lowest possible tax rate.

Switching accountants

It has been my experience that many business owners put up with a substandard accountant for a lot longer than they should. This may be a reflection of the Australian dislike for complaining, or it could be caused by a belief that a new accountant would find it too hard to understand how the business works. If you hold this belief, don't delay looking for a new accountant—any good accountant should be able to easily take over the financial and tax affairs of a business after looking at its most recent financial and tax information.

If you do decide that you want to change your accountant, a good way to start looking is to talk with business associates. In most cases it should not take long to get a recommendation of an accountant who will work with you to help improve and grow your business.

If you cannot get a recommendation for a new accountant, phone one and ask for an initial meeting. Someone who does not ask many questions, and is not interested in your business or the way it is organised, is probably a tax agent. If, on the other hand, the person asks lots of questions, seems interested in what your business does, and offers some preliminary ways to improve your situation, he or she will more than likely be an accountant, and worth using.

CHAPTER 15

Questions and answers

This last chapter is devoted to questions from readers of *The Age* that represent some common concerns and worries. Skim through to find the questions that will be relevant to and helpful for you, with the answers.

GST questions

Can GST be claimed without a tax invoice?

Q I need your response to a question regarding the charging of GST on invoices for the supply of goods and services. Can you advise how, in the absence of a legal tax invoice, this can be done and also how the payer can claim the GST paid as a credit if they do not have a tax invoice?

A To be able to claim a credit for GST paid, a business must be in possession of a tax invoice that has all the prescribed details.

Professional artist

Q I am a professional artist. I sell my paintings through exhibitions run by Rotary clubs, schools and through art galleries. I pay GST on painting equipment, entry fees to exhibitions, frames and courier services. How can I have my GST costs refunded?

A To be able to claim a refund of GST paid you must be registered for GST. If you do not register for GST, you will not be able to claim a refund. All businesses that earn more than $75 000 a year are required to register for GST; and any business earning less than $75 000 can elect to register. Once you're registered for GST you will be required to charge GST on the paintings you sell. The only time you get a refund of GST paid is when it is greater than GST collected by you.

When you sell your paintings through an agent, such as Rotary, there will be two lots of GST payable. GST will be charged to the person who buys the painting, and the agent will charge GST on the commission he or she takes. For example, if you were not registered for GST and sold a painting for $500, and the agent charged $55 in commission, you would net $455. If you were registered for GST, $50 would be added on to the price of the painting, making a total selling price of $550. You would receive $495, made up of the $550 selling price less $55 in commission. You would then have to pay $45 in GST on to the tax office. This is made up of the $50 GST collected less the $5 paid on the commission.

Body corporate

Q I am the honorary secretary of an eight-unit body corporate. We pay $75 a quarter, which covers security lighting, cutting of lawns and our insurance cover. If there is a shortfall, we make a special levy to cover it. Could you please tell me what effect GST has on our body corporate?

A From the information you have provided, the annual turnover of the body corporate would be under $75 000.

Any entity with a turnover of less than $75000 does not have to register for GST. Where an entity does not register for GST it does not charge GST on the income it earns. As a consequence, it does not get a credit for the GST it pays.

In your case, GST paid on things like insurance, lawnmowing and the electricity bill could not be claimed as a credit, as you would not have charged GST. If you decided to register for GST, however, this situation would change, as a body corporate administering residential accommodation would charge GST on its services. The body corporate would claim a credit of GST it paid, which would be offset against GST it collected.

Services provided to an overseas company

Q I provide inspection services to shipping companies; most of my work is done by contracts with foreign shipping classification agencies. One of those agencies is based in Germany but operates through an Australian subsidiary company with an office in Sydney. The ships I inspect are mainly foreign-owned and registered, therefore the classification agencies are billing overseas companies. The agency bills the shipping companies and advises me how much my fee is.

My questions are:

(a) If I can only bill what I am advised, and am not able to increase the bill for GST, does that mean I must effectively take a reduction in income?

(b) I have heard that export industries do not have to charge GST. If that were the case would that mean, by billing the German agency direct, I would not have to charge GST?

A Yes, you would earn less income as a result of not being able to increase your fee. For example if you had to bill the agency $550 including GST, you would have to pay $50 in GST and receive only $500.

Export industries are classed as GST-free industries. That means they do not have to charge GST but they get a refund of the GST they pay. If your client has an Australian subsidiary, and your contract is with the subsidiary, you would be regarded as rendering a service to a resident Australian company and not providing a GST-free service.

In this case your charge would have to increase by 10 per cent for the GST. The bill charged to the overseas shipping company by the Australian subsidiary would be GST-free and no GST would be included. The Australian subsidiary would get a credit for the GST charged by you, so their costs would not increase.

In short, if your contract is with the German company, and you bill it direct, you would be rendering a GST-free service and would not have to charge GST. If the Australian subsidiary billed the foreign shipping company, it would still be rendering a GST-free service and would not have to charge GST.

Doctors and GST-free status

Q With the claiming of tax credits of GST paid on supplies and services: how will a doctor who is GST exempt be able to claim the tax credits? The doctor is unable to charge the 10 percent GST on his or her services.

A No-one is exempt from GST. Everyone pays GST on nearly all of the things they buy. The services provided by doctors are in the main classed as GST-free. This means that doctors do not charge GST on medically necessary treatment. The sort of treatment that would not be classed as medically necessary is plastic surgery to improve someone's appearance.

Anyone who provides GST-free services does not charge GST, but gets a credit for any GST they pay. Most businesses with a turnover of less than $20 million can pay the GST collected on a quarterly basis. Businesses can also elect to report GST on a monthly basis if they want to. Doctors, and other providers of GST-free services such as dentists, should choose the monthly method of reporting if their PAYG instalments are less than the GST refund.

What is included in business income?

Q As a civil celebrant I expect my yearly income to be below $75 000. However, with interest, dividends and an allocated pension added to this income, I could be well over the $75 000. Which part or parts of my income counts towards the $75 000 limit? If I do not have to register for GST, should I register? At what point would I need to register and start charging GST?

A In calculating your yearly income for GST purposes, you only have to take into account your business income. Your investment income and allocated pension income is not included for GST purposes. You should only register for GST if you will be paying a reasonable amount of GST on the costs associated with your business. In your case, I do not think you will be paying much GST.

As your customers would not be able to get a credit for any GST charged by you, the cost of your services would increase by the GST charged, so there is no benefit for your customers if you register for GST.

Subcontractors and registering for GST

Q My wife and I operate a small partnership that coordinates
the delivery of junk mail. We receive bundles of pamphlets
from various persons and then arrange the delivery
to letterboxes. We have a team of about 50 part-time
subcontractors who deliver the mail. No tax is deducted
from the payments I receive from my suppliers, and I
do not deduct tax from the deliverers. My net income is
derived from the difference between the price I charge
the suppliers and what I pay the deliverers. Our income
will soon exceed $75 000. Can you briefly explain my
GST position?

A Before explaining how the GST system affects you, I
should start with your current obligations under the PAYG
withholding system. When you pay someone for work
they do for you, like delivering junk mail, you should be
treating them as an employee and deducting tax from the
amount paid. The only way that this can be avoided is if
the people contract to you through a company. You are not
only be liable to deduct tax under the PAYG system, but
you are also liable to pay WorkCover and super guarantee
contributions for the people working for you.

As your turnover will be exceeding $75 000, you will
have to register for GST. If your deliverers provided their
services through a company that is registered for GST, they
will already be charging you GST on the amount billed to
you. You, in turn, will have to charge your suppliers GST
on the amount you bill them. For example, on a delivery
fee of $3000 charged to a supplier, you would need to
charge $300 GST. If a subcontracting company charged
you $1100, including $100 in GST, you would have to pay
$200 to the tax office on that transaction.

The difference between commercial and residential leases

Q Can you please confirm how rent is treated under GST? With commercial premises, does the tenant pay the 10 per cent extra with the rent payment? With residential premises is the procedure still the same?

A GST on rent differs between commercial and residential premises. When an owner of a commercial property is registered, or required to be registered, for GST, the rent charged must have GST included. Residential property, however, is classed as input-taxed and does not have GST included.

Who pays GST on commercial property?

Q I am about to purchase two shops. The rent from the one leased to a pizza operator is $45 000 and the rent from the one leased to a photocopy business is $40 000. Do I have to register for GST? Who pays it?

A As both shops are commercial premises, and your income will be greater than $75 000, you must register for GST and include it in the rent. If the tenants are also registered for GST they will get a credit for it. If they are not registered for GST no credit can be claimed.

GST and a property that's part commercial and part residential

Q My wife owns a shop with a separate dwelling. The shop is let, and my wife and I occupy the dwelling. She is registered for GST. I am not sure what should happen when she sells the property.

A Where someone is registered for GST and they sell a property, GST would have to be included in the price when it is sold. There are two methods that can be used to calculate GST payable on properties sold. The amount of GST payable will be either 10 per cent of the selling price, or one-eleventh of the increase in the value of the property after 1 July 2000 to the date of sale. In most cases, the second method will give the lowest GST payable, but the purchaser will not be entitled to an input tax credit if this method is adopted.

In addition, the valuation would need to have separate values placed on the business premises and the residence. Residential premises, excluding new premises, do not have GST charged on their sale; the sale of commercial premises do attract GST where the seller is involved in buying and selling properties and is registered for GST.

Selling a farm but not registered for GST

Q My wife and I own a small farm that we plan to sell. The income from the farm has always been below the threshold for GST, and so we have not charged or claimed GST in the past. When we sell the property, are we required to charge GST?

A Because you are not registered for GST you will not have to charge GST on the farm when you sell it.

Superannuation questions

Investing versus making super contributions

Q I operate a business through a company and pay tax at the top marginal rate of 46.5 per cent. I can either take the profits out of the company, pay tax and invest in my name, or I can keep the profit in the company and invest it there. If the investment yields income of 4 per cent and a capital gain of 6 per cent per annum for 10 years, am I better off to investment in the company or in my own name?

A Being on the top marginal tax rate, if you took a $10 000 dividend from the company, after paying tax and getting an imputation credit, you would be left with $7643. Over a 10-year period, reinvesting the income, your capital gain would be $6688. After the 50 per cent general discount and paying tax at 46.5 per cent, you would be left with $15 161.

If, instead, the $10 000 was left in the company and invested, the capital gain would be $9029. If $10 000 plus the accumulated income and capital gain were paid to you as a dividend, you would be left with $15 694 after paying tax on the dividend.

In addition to those two options, there are two others based around superannuation. Your first option would be to make the after-tax dividend a non-concessional contribution to a super fund. If this was invested for the same 10-year period, you would be left with $16 496 if you took the amount as a lump sum before turning 60, and $18 769 if you waited until turning 60.

An even better option would be to make a deductible super contribution of $10 000 that would save the company $3000 in tax. After paying the contribution tax, the super fund would be left with $8500 to invest. Over the 10 years, this would result in you receiving $17 071 before turning 60 and $20 873 if you received the payout after turning 60.

Proof for the work test

Q The work test requires 40 hours in one month a year minimum: what proof is required by the ATO that 40 hours' work occurred in one month?

A Most super funds require members in this situation to sign a declaration that they have passed the work test. If you have a self managed super fund (SMSF), or are contacted by the ATO, your proof could be in the form of a PAYG withholding summary, a pay slip, a bank record of the amount paid and the hourly rate earned, or anything else that demonstrates you actually worked the required hours.

Leasing equipment from a super fund

Q I run a business that requires additional computer hardware at a cost of approximately $80 000. I have ample cash deposits in my super fund, and would get a better return by buying the equipment and leasing it to my business on commercial terms. Is there any reason why my business can't lease the equipment from the super fund?

A. Under the regulations, a super fund cannot provide finance to a member or related person or entity. This means it cannot provide lease finance for the computer equipment you require. The only exception is the in-house asset rule: under this rule, a super fund can have up to 5 per cent of its value as in-house assets. For your SMSF to provide the lease finance, you would need to have at least $1.6 million in your fund.

Self-employed and setting up a SMSF

Q I have been self-employed for the last 22 years and I am anticipating retiring within a year or two. I have now turned 60 and I have just started my own self managed super fund. I have rolled over about $600 000 into the fund from other super funds I had. I am intending to invest this money, but I am not clear if I have to pay tax on any subsequent profits my super fund makes after investing this money.

A If your superannuation fund is not paying you a pension, tax will be payable on all income and capitals gains. Tax is paid at 15 per cent on income and contributions, while capital gains are taxed at 10 per cent. If you buy shares, tax is only paid on the gain when they are sold, not on their increase in value each year. A super fund that pays a pension does not pay tax. If you started a 'transition to retirement pension', the pension would be tax-free, and the super fund would not pay tax on the income earned and capital gains made.

What is compulsory super payable on?

Q Do employers have to pay super on gross weekly wages including weekend work? Our accountant thought that super did not need be paid on Sunday work.

A Under the superannuation guarantee rules, an employer must make a super contribution of 9 per cent on an employee's ordinary earnings. In your case, if you worked on Sundays as part of your usual hours, your employer should make a super contribution on those wages. If your Sunday work is regarded as overtime, however, your employer would not have to make a super contribution.

Making undeducted contributions

Q I have a long-established SMSF paying an allocated pension, with my daughter as co-trustee. My daughter has her own fund with her husband, but I would like to make her a member of my fund and make annual undeducted contributions on her behalf to my fund. Is this possible?

A As long as your daughter is either under 65 or, if 65 or older, satisfies the work test, you could have her become a member of your super fund and make undeducted contributions on her behalf. You must ensure that the undeducted contributions made by you, when combined with any made to her SMSF, do not exceed the annual or three-year undeducted limits.

PAYG instalments and superannuation pension income

Q I continue getting quarterly ATO requests for PAYG income tax instalments. I was under the impression that, as our SMSF pays a pension to my wife and myself, and we are both over 70, it and we do not pay any tax after 1 July 2007. I have been told by the ATO that only my pension, not my SMSF, was tax-free even though 72 per cent of it consists of a complying pension. Am I getting incorrect advice from ATO?

A If your only source of income is a superannuation pension, you will not be paying tax from 1 July this year. As such you should not be paying any further PAYG tax instalments. If your super fund has 28 per cent of its investments in accumulation phase, however, it will still pay tax on the income this part of your fund earns, and therefore may have to pay PAYG instalments. No tax will be payable by the fund on income earned by the investments used to fund the pension.

How to invest for retirement

Q I have recently turned 60 and am a widow with two adult children who are not married. I would like to help them financially by setting up a share portfolio, so that they could buy their first homes in the future. This would leave me with about $200 000. How do you suggest I invest the money for my retirement? I intend to work until I am 70 years old. I pay tax at 15 per cent and currently work 38 hours per week. I have about $20 000 in an employer super fund.

A When you have money to invest, you need to choose what you are going to invest in. Your options are cash, fixed interest, property, Australian shares and overseas shares. As each of these investments carry with them different levels of investor risk, it is important that you have a mix of them.

The percentage you have in each class of investment will depend on your tolerance to risk. The more you are likely to worry about losing money, the less you should have in the share area. You should also not be fooled into thinking that fixed-interest investments are safe. These investments, such as bonds, can suffer decreases in value, especially in an environment of rising interest rates or as has been experienced with the subprime crisis in the USA.

In addition, it is important to understand that not all property investments are the same. Some property investments are listed on the stock exchange, and their value can fluctuate due to market sentiment or other factors, such as occurred with the subprime fiasco. Other property trusts are unlisted, and their value is more directly tied to the underlying value of the properties they have invested in.

Before deciding on your mix of investments, however, you need to decide on how you are going to invest the $200 000. If you invest in your own name, a portion of the investment income may be taxed at only 15 per cent, but some may be taxed at 30 per cent. So, you should think about investing through a superannuation fund.

By investing through a super fund, the investment income will be taxed at no more than 15 per cent. If you decide that you need extra income, you could commence a 'transition to retirement pension'. Once you start drawing this tax-free income, the super fund goes from accumulation phase to pension phase, so it would also not pay any tax.

By starting a pension, you would end up with two super accounts: your pension account and a new accumulation account to receive your employer's contributions and any new contributions you make.

Instead of investing all of the $200 000 in one lump sum, keep approximately $20 000 to invest over the next 10 years until you turn 70. This will mean you have a reserve of cash should you need it. In addition, by making non-concessional contributions over the next 10 years your investment will be boosted by the Commonwealth superannuation co-contribution.

To be eligible for the co-contribution you must be under 71, earn 10 per cent or more of your income from employment, and have income of less than $58 980. If your assessable income was less than $28 980 and you contributed at least $1000 a year as a non-concessional contribution, you would receive $1500 a year from the government.

Before taking any action, seek the help of a financial adviser. To ensure you get the right advice and don't pay too much, try and find an adviser who charges a fee instead of commissions.

Capital gains questions

Carried forward company loss and capital gain

Q I have a company with a $40 000 carried forward tax loss. Our accountant tells us that we cannot offset this loss against capital gains on the sale of a property. Is this correct?

A A capital gain in a company is treated as taxable income. To this is added the other income for the year, and then deductible expenses are subtracted. If there is a taxable net income left carried forward, losses are deducted from this figure. Any income left is taxed at the company rate. If there is still a loss, this is carried forward to later years.

Reducing a capital gain using super contribution

Q I have a self managed super fund which is in the pension phase, and substantial assets outside the fund, and I recently sold a property, realising a capital gain of about $100 000. I have been told that if I go back to work for at least 40 hours in a 30-day period, I can make a tax-deductible contribution to my super fund of $100 000 per calendar year until 2012. Is this correct?

A If you are 65 or older, you must pass the 40-hour work test to be able to make super contributions. To claim a tax deduction for a personal super contribution, your income from employment must be less than 10 per cent of your total income in the year you make the contribution.

Capital gain on gift of shares

Q Can capital gains tax be avoided by gifting shares to relatives before you die?

A Even when you give an asset away, it is still caught as a capital gains tax event. In your case, tax would be payable on the discounted difference between the market value of the shares on the day of the gift and what the shares cost.

Capital gain and receiving a super pension

Q I am 62 and am aware that if I retire I can withdraw any amount from my superannuation tax-free. Can I work one day a week and still be considered 'retired' for this purpose? Also, if I have a CGT liability of $30 000, is this added to my total gross income for the year regardless of whether I am working or not?

A For people between the ages of 59 and 65, the conditions that must be met to access super are simpler than for those who are younger. Once a person turns 65, the only condition of release required is that they cease employment. This can either be through resigning, being made redundant or being fired.

This means if you only have one job you would have to resign from it. You could however find other employment, even a part-time position, and then resign from that. This would mean you could continue with you current employer but still get access to your superannuation.

When a capital gain is made, the assessable portion is added to your other taxable income. For example, if you had employment income of $35 000, an exempt super pension of $15 000, and the capital gain of $30 000, your total taxable income would be $65 000. Tax would be payable on the capital gain at 30 per cent, resulting in tax of $10 500.

Avoiding capital gains on investment property

Q If superannuation funds are allowed to buy and sell investments whilst super contributions are being made, without paying capital gains tax, can property owners claim the same exemption when buying and selling property which forms part of their retirement planning?

A Superannuation funds in accumulation stage, when contributions are still being made, do pay tax. However, it is paid at only 15 per cent on income and 10 per cent on capital gains. It is only when a super fund starts to pay a pension that it ceases paying both income and capital gains tax. A person who uses property as a means of saving for their retirement gets taxed normally.

Since *Simple Super* was introduced, people using property as a de facto form of superannuation can be seriously disadvantaged. Once they start using the property income to fund their retirement, they pay tax on their retirement income at normal tax rates, apart from a few rebates open to all people over 65. People in this situation should seek advice on how they can tax-effectively move from having their retirement investments in property, into having money invested through superannuation.

Pre–capital gains tax assets and death

Q My wife's father died in 1981, pre CGT. He left shares held in trust for his wife, who received the dividends but could not sell them. When she died last year the shares were distributed by her executor, in accord with his will, to the sons and daughters. Am I right in thinking that no CGT would be payable on the sale of these shares?

A In normal circumstances, when a person sells an asset purchased before 19 September 1985 no capital gains tax is payable. If the asset sold was purchased after that date, CGT is payable on 50 per cent of the gain if the asset has been owned for more than 12 months.

The exception to this is when assets are received from a deceased's estate. Assets inherited before 19 September 1985 are not subject to CGT. The tax treatment of assets inherited after that date will depend on when the original owner purchased them.

If the deceased purchased the asset after 19 September 1985, the cost for CGT purposes for the person inheriting the asset will be the same as the person who died and originally bought it. Where the asset was purchased by the deceased before 19 September 1985, the cost to the person inheriting them will be their market value at the date of death.

When a person receives assets from the estate of someone who died before 19 September 1985, they are regarded as having inherited a pre-CGT asset. In your situation, as your father-in-law died in 1981, the shares inherited by your wife are a pre-CGT asset. This will mean no tax will be payable when they are sold.

Accumulated individual loss and capital gain

Q I have accumulated a capital loss of $10 000 in my tax account over the years. I have made a $5000 capital gain this year that would not be taxable, as my total income is too low. Must I offset the capital gain in the current tax year against losses accumulated over past years?

A When it comes to normal capital gains (those not related to the small business CGT exemptions), there is a strict order laid down on how a gain must be treated. After the capital gain has been calculated on the sale of an asset, it is first reduced by any capital losses made in the same year from the sale of other assets. The resulting capital gain must then be reduced by any accumulated capital losses brought forward from previous years. This reduced capital gain amount is then reduced, if the asset was owned for at least 12 months, by the general 50 per cent discount.

In your case, the capital gain of $5000 will be reduced to nil by offsetting $5000 of your carried forward capital losses. This will leave you with no reportable capital gain this year and $5000 of capital losses to carry forward to future years.

Appendix

Table 1: tax rates for individuals

Taxable income threshold	Tax payable	Plus tax on excess
2007–08		
$0 to $6000	Nil	Zero
$6001 to $30 000	Nil	15 per cent
$30 001 to $75 000	$3600	30 per cent
$75 001 to $150 000	$17 100	40 per cent
$150 001 and over	$47 100	45 per cent
2008–09		
$0 to $6000	Nil	Zero
$6001 to $34 000	Nil	15 per cent
$34 001 to $80 000	$4200	30 per cent
$80 001 to $180 000	$18 000	40 per cent
$180 001 and over	$58 000	45 per cent
2009–10		
$0 to $6000	Nil	Zero
$6001 to $35 000	Nil	15 per cent
$35 001 to $80 000	$4350	30 per cent
$80 001 to $180 000	$17 850	38 per cent
$180 001 and over	$55 850	45 per cent
2010–11		
$0 to $6000	Nil	Zero
$6001 to $37 000	Nil	15 per cent
$37 001 to $80 000	$4650	30 per cent
$80 001 to $180 000	$17 550	37 per cent
$180 001 and over	$54 550	45 per cent

Table 2: tax paid on income distributed to children under 18

Taxable income threshold	Tax payable	Plus tax on excess
$416	Nil	Zero
$417 to $1455	Nil	66 per cent

Where income exceeds $1455, tax is paid on the whole amount at 45 per cent.

Company tax rate

30 per cent on all net taxable income.

Table 3: Medicare levy taxable income thresholds 2006–07

	No levy	Reduced levy	1.5% levy
Single taxpayers			
	$16740	$16741 to $19694	$19694
Married taxpayers with number of children or students			
0	$28247	$28248 to $33231	$33231
1	$30841	$30842 to $36283	$36283
2	$33435	$33436 to $39335	$39335
3	$36029	$36030 to $42387	$42387
4	$38623	$38624 to $45438	$45438

* Medicare levy is payable at 1.5 per cent on all income once taxable income threshold is exceeded.

* The thresholds for married couples apply to the joint income of the family.

* Sole parents who receive either the sole parent or housekeeper rebates use the married threshold.

* For each extra child over four, the shading-in threshold increases by $2594, and by $3051 for the full levy threshold.

* For those people eligible to receive a senior Australian or pensioner tax offset, the thresholds are higher.

Table 4: Medicare surcharge taxable income thresholds

Single taxpayers

$50000

Married taxpayers with number of children or students

0	$100000
1	$100000
2	$101500
3	$103000
4	$104500

Where taxpayers do not have private health insurance and their income exceeds the relevant threshold above, they pay the Medicare surcharge of 1 per cent. For each extra child or student, the threshold is increased by $1500. Note that these thresholds could change as a result of the 2008 Budget to $100000 for individuals and $150000 for families.

Table 5: tax offsets

There are several tax offsets, or 'rebates' as they were once called, that reduce the amount of tax a person pays. The most common offsets applicable to small business owners are given below with their income thresholds and cut-off thresholds.

	Amount	Threshold	Cut-off
Dependent spouse offset	$2100	$282	$8682
Low income offset	$750	$30000	$48750
Mature age worker offset	$500	$5000	$63000
Senior Australian offset			
Single	$2230	$24867	$42707
Member of a couple	$1602	$20680	$33496
Medical expenses over $1500	20 per cent		
Entrepreneurs' offset*	25 per cent		

* See chapter 3 for a full description.

Table 6: minimum superannuation pension rates

Age of super fund member	Minimum pension rate
55 to 64	4 per cent
65 to 74	5 per cent
75 to 79	6 per cent
80 to 84	7 per cent
85 to 89	9 per cent
90 to 94	11 per cent
95 and over	14 per cent

Table 7: when you can access your super

Age	Conditions
65 and over	No conditions, super can be accessed at any time
60 to 64	Termination of employment
55 to 59	Transition to retirement pension
	Retiring and not intending to work more than 10 hours a week
18 to 65	Severe financial hardship
	Terminal illness
	Compassionate grounds
	Permanent incapacity
	Temporary incapacity
	Death
	Departing Australia permanently
All ages	Death or to pay excess contributions tax

Table 8: taxation of lump sum super payments

Age of person receiving the payment	Tax rate
60 and over	Nil
55 to 59	
Up to tax-free threshold — $140 000 for 2007–08	Nil
Excess over tax-free threshold	15 per cent
Under 55	20 per cent
Permanent invalidity payments	Nil
Temporary invalidity payments	Marginal tax rate
Death benefits	
To dependants	Nil
To non-dependants	15 per cent

Table 9: tax payable on superannuation pensions

Age of person receiving pension	Tax rate
60 and over	Nil
55 to 59	Marginal rate less 15 per cent super pension rebate
Under 55	Marginal tax rate
Permanent invalidity payments	Nil
Temporary invalidity payments	Marginal tax rate
Death benefits	
To dependants over 60	Nil
To dependants under 60	Marginal rate less 15 per cent super pension rebate

Table 10: maximum super contributions

Age person turns during:	2007–08	2008–09	2009–10	2010–11	2011–12	2012–13
50 and over	$100 000	$100 000	$100 000	$100 000	$100 000	$50 000
49	$50 000	$100 000	$100 000	$100 000	$100 000	$50 000
48	$50 000	$50 000	$100 000	$100 000	$100 000	$50 000
47	$50 000	$50 000	$50 000	$100 000	$100 000	$50 000
46	$50 000	$50 000	$50 000	$50 000	$100 000	$50 000
45 and younger	$50 000	$50 000	$50 000	$50 000	$50 000	$50 000

Note: the minimum $50 000 increases in line with AWOTE (average weekly ordinary times earnings) in amounts of $5000.

Table 11: statutory car FBT rates

Total km driven in a year	FBT rate applied to cost of car
Less than 15 000	26 per cent
15 000 to 24 999	20 per cent
25 000 to 39 999	11 per cent
40 000 and over	7 per cent

Table 12: kilometre rates for claiming cars 2006–07

Conventional engine	Rotary engine	Cents per km
Up to 1600cc	Up to 800cc	58 cents
1601cc to 2600cc	801cc to 1300cc	69 cents
Over 2600cc	Over 1300cc	70 cents

Table 13: GST claimable on car costs under statutory method

Km driven	Percentage of GST claimable
1 to 1250	5 per cent
1251 to 2500	10 per cent
2501 to 3750	15 per cent
3751 to 5000	20 per cent

Table 14: write-off of assets under the SBE tax system

Asset cost	Deductible amount	
	First year	*Subsequent*
Less than $1000 net of GST	100 per cent	
More than $1000 net of GST, pooled:		
With expected useful life of <25 years	15 per cent	30 per cent
With expected useful life of 25 years+	2.50 per cent	5 per cent

Note: 'assets with expected useful life of 25 years+' does not include buildings.

GST-free goods and services

GST-free goods and services comprise:

- medical services (includes items covered by Medicare)
- health services such as physio, dental and optical
- medical appliances, drugs and medicines
- residential and community care for the aged
- cars for use by disabled people
- educational courses and most materials
- eligible child care
- religious services and charitable activities
- water and sewerage charges
- exports
- first supply of precious metals after refining
- subdivided farm land (conditions apply)
- sales to overseas tourists (duty-free shops)
- sale of a business as a going concern
- basic foods.

GST-free and GST-payable food

GST is included in the price of:

- takeaway food — including prepared sandwiches, rolls and fruit platters
- restaurant meals
- alcohol
- soft drinks and cordials
- flavoured milk
- snack foods
- confectionary
- cakes, muffins, pies
- bakery products (except bread).

GST is not included in the price of:

- bread
- meat and processed meat
- fruit and vegetables — fresh, canned, dried and frozen
- fruit juice with 90 per cent or more of juice
- cereals
- coffee, tea and sugar
- flour
- dairy products, including milk and cheese
- poultry and seafood
- eggs
- dried pasta, rice and grains
- other basic food items such as soup.

Input-taxed goods and services

No GST is charged on:

- bank charges
- lender's mortgage insurance
- loans
- life insurance
- hire-purchase
- shares
- superannuation funds
- rent and sale of residential premises.

GST is charged on:

- credit card merchant fees
- legal services
- accounting services
- insurances (other than life insurance)
- tax agents' fees
- payroll services
- leases.

GST norms method

To be able to use the GST norms method, a business must:

- be registered for GST
- qualify as an SBE with turnover of $2 million or less
- not have point-of-sale equipment that can identify and record a mix of taxable and GST-free sales
- sell taxable and GST-free food from the same premises.

In addition, each category has some other requirements and the rates differ.

Convenience store operator

- sells milk, bread, soft drinks, cigarettes, confectionery, ice-cream or groceries
- does not sell fuel or alcoholic beverages
- converts GST-free food into taxable food (for example, prepares hamburgers or sandwiches).

GST-free sales — 22.5 per cent
GST-free purchases — 30 per cent

Convenience store operator

- sells milk, bread, soft drinks, cigarettes, confectionery, ice-cream or groceries
- does not sell fuel or alcoholic beverages
- only resells products and does not prepare taxable food, such as hamburgers, from GST-free ingredients.

GST-free sales — 30 per cent
GST-free purchases — 30 per cent

Rural convenience store operator

- sells taxable and GST-free food from the same premises
- does not sell alcoholic beverages
- has a net simplified GST turnover of $2 million or less after deducting any fuel sales and Australia Post agency business.

Before applying the business norms percentages, you must deduct any fuel or Australia Post agency business sales from total sales, then deduct any fuel or Australia Post agency business purchases from total purchases.

For a store that converts GST-free food into GST-payable food, such as bread and fillings into sandwiches or GST-free potatoes and fish into taxable fish and chips:

GST-free sales — 22.5 per cent
GST-free purchases — 30 per cent

For a store that doesn't convert food or prepare takeaways or hot food:

GST-free sales — 30 per cent
GST-free purchases — 30 per cent

Hot bread shop

A store that mainly sells bread (as opposed to shops that specialise in cakes):

GST-free sales — 50 per cent
GST-free purchases — 75 per cent

Cake shop operator

A store that mainly sells cakes, pastries or similar products, and does not operate as a café:

GST-free sales — 2 per cent
GST-free purchases — 95 per cent

Appendix

Fresh fish retailer
A store that mainly sells fresh fish and other seafood, with some sales of cooked fish and chips (does not mainly sell cooked fish and chips):

> GST-free sales — 35 per cent
> GST-free purchases — 98 per cent

Health food shop operator
A store that sells food, food supplements, vitamins and other health food products, and does not convert GST-free food into taxable foods (for example, doesn't prepare sandwiches or make health food bars):

> GST-free sales — 35 per cent
> GST-free purchases — 35 per cent

Continental delicatessen operator
- mainly sells processed meats, smallgoods, salamis, cheeses and similar items
- does not sell mostly grocery items, even if the store is known as a 'deli' or delicatessen
- does not make any café or restaurant sales.

> GST-free sales — 85 per cent
> GST-free purchases — 90 per cent

Pharmacy operator with dispensary sales
A store that has dispensary sales (for example, claimable NHS prescriptions), non-claimable private prescriptions

and over-the-counter (OTC) sales, including food sales. The GST norms method can be used even if dispensary systems (with shopfront point-of-sale equipment) can identify and record dispensary sales for claimable NHS prescriptions.

You must deduct the patient contribution for claimable NHS prescriptions from your total amount of sales (which your shopfront point-of-sale equipment has recorded), identify the non-claimable dispensary and OTC components of your sales, and then apply the relevant business norms percentages to each component.

Dispensary non-claimable

GST-free sales — 98 per cent

GST-free purchases — 0 per cent

Over the counter

GST-free sales — 47.5 per cent

GST-free purchases — 2 per cent

Glossary

Active asset An asset used in the carrying on of a business, such as business premises, plant and equipment, or an intangible asset connected with the business such as goodwill or trademarks.

Aggregated turnover The total turnover for a business, including all entities such as companies, trusts and other individuals that are controlled or connected with a taxpayer.

ATO Australian Taxation Office.

Australian business number (ABN) The Australian business number is an identification number that was introduced as part of the GST system. Where an entity does not quote an ABN in its business dealings with a registered business, tax must be deducted at 48.5 per cent.

Average weekly ordinary times earnings (AWOTE) AWOTE is the average of full-time adult weekly ordinary time earnings for all persons in Australia. It excludes overtime earned. The increase in this average is a benchmark used when increasing various government thresholds, including those related to superannuation.

Bona fide redundancy payments These are payments by an employer to an employee who has been made redundant. For a person to be redundant, the position he or she previously worked in cannot be given to another employee.

Business activity statement (BAS) The business activity statement is a tax reporting system designed to streamline and condense all forms of tax reporting. The taxes covered by the BAS include GST, fringe benefits tax, tax file number withholding tax, PAYG group tax, and instalments of income tax. The BAS allows businesses to send off one payment covering all of the different taxes that must be paid to the tax office.

Capital gains tax (CGT) The system introduced on 20 September 1985 that taxed profits made on all assets and investments, with only a few exceptions.

Capital gains tax–exempt Some assets do not have capital gains tax paid on them. These include assets purchased before 19 September 1985 and a person's home.

Carrying on an enterprise An enterprise is an activity carried on by an entity; something done in the form of a business for the ultimate purpose of making a profit. To understand what an enterprise is, you should appreciate what is not classed as an enterprise. The things excluded are:

- activities done as an employee, a company director, under a labour hire arrangement, or as a member of a state, territory, council or authority
- hobbies and private recreational pursuits
- activities done without a reasonable expectation of earning a profit, such as hobby farming.

Complying superannuation fund A superannuation fund that meets all of the relevant government standards set out in the *Superannuation (Industry) Supervision Act 1993*, and that has elected to be regulated under the Act. A complying superannuation fund is eligible for concessional tax treatment.

Condition of release One of the conditions laid down by law that enables a person to access their superannuation. The conditions of release are based on a person's age, employment status, and other circumstances specified in the SIS Act.

Consideration The value that is received when a transaction takes place. It can take the form of money; it can also be in the form of goods or services exchanged or the use of which is allowed. For example, a plumber who clears the drains of a property owner may be given the use of a holiday house for a weekend in return. The value in this case would be what the house would have been normally rented for.

Creditable purpose When something is purchased by an enterprise in the carrying on of its business, it has been purchased for a 'creditable purpose'. In other words, the GST paid on the purchase can be claimed as a credit. The exceptions to this rule are:
- when the business is making input-taxed supplies
- when the item purchased is not tax-deductible (such as customer entertaining or where the item is for private use).

Deductible contributions Super contributions made by employers or self-employed people, including salary sacrifice super contributions. A tax benefit is obtained when these contributions are made: this depends on who makes the contributions, but varies between zero and 30 per cent for individuals and zero and 15 per cent for companies. The tax benefit is the difference between the tax rate paid by the person or entity making the contribution and the 15 per cent tax rate paid by a super fund.

Enterprise An enterprise is a business that is carried on for the purpose of making a profit. It does not include hobbies. It does include the activities of charities, government and religious organisations, deductible gift recipients and certain non-profit organisations.

Entity An 'entity' can be an individual, a partnership, a trust, a company, charity, co-operative, super fund, body corporate, and so on.

Fringe benefits tax (FBT) A system brought in to tax benefits taken by employees in forms other than salaries or wages.

General interest charge (GIC) The penalty levied by the ATO in the form of interest when tax is underpaid.

Goods and services tax (GST) The goods and services tax system, introduced on 1 July 2000 to broaden the tax base instead of just concentrating on income. It replaced the complicated sales tax system that previously existed.

GST-free goods and services One of only three classifications of goods and services for GST purposes. This particular classification covers the necessities of life, such as education, essential medical services, food, health services, prescription drugs and medicines, child care, water and sewerage, and aged residential care. The export of goods and services is also considered GST-free. Businesses do not have to charge GST on GST-free goods and services, but get a credit for any GST paid on inputs incurred in earning the GST-free income.

GST-taxed goods and services The category of goods and services that most businesses supply or sell. If you run a business and you do not have a good or service that is in the GST-free or input-taxed categories you are in the GST-taxed category. GST is charged on the supply of all GST-taxed goods and services, and a credit is allowed for all GST paid on business inputs.

Income tax The tax paid on the net taxable income earned by individuals, companies, super funds and so on.

Incurred This is a term that has two meanings, depending on whether the cash or accrual method of accounting is used. Under the cash method, 'incurred' means when something is paid. Under the accrual method, 'incurred' means when you have a liability to pay for something — for example, when goods are received from a supplier on credit or something has been purchased using a credit card.

Inputs These are the costs that a business pays in earning its income. Some inputs are directly related to the earning of income, such as the cost of goods sold. Other inputs are more general, such as the overhead of renting business premises. Where a business earns different sorts of GST income, it must apportion its input costs between each type of income.

Input tax credits A business that earns GST-taxed and GST-free income can claim a credit for the 10 per cent GST paid on all of its business inputs. The total of all input tax credits can be used to decrease the amount of GST collected that must be paid to the tax office. The input tax credits can also be used to produce a refund where they are greater than the GST collected.

Input-taxed goods and services Input-taxed goods and services include financial products such as loans, leases, shares and managed investments. They also include life insurance, but not include other types of insurance. A business making an input-taxed supply does not charge GST and does not get a credit for GST paid on inputs incurred in earning the supply.

Net amount payable or creditable When a business completes its BAS it is either due for a refund of GST or it has to pay GST. In the majority of cases, businesses have a net amount payable because the GST charged and collected is greater than the GST they have paid.

Net capital gain This is the amount of a capital gain made on the sale of an asset that must be included in assessable income. It is the gain remaining after deducting any applicable concessions, such as the 50 per cent general concession or any of the small business CGT concessions

Pay as you go (PAYG) This system was created when GST was introduced in 2000. It requires employers to deduct tax from employees, PAYG withholding, and requires the self-employed and investors to pay tax over the course of a year called PAYG instalment system.

Retirement exemption A tax exemption available to qualifying taxpayers for capital gains made on the sale of active business assets.

SBE A business that qualifies as a small business entity.

Self-employed A person who does not have any superannuation contributions made on his or her behalf by an employer, or only has very minor employer superannuation contributions from an employer.

Self managed super fund (SMSF) A super fund regulated by the ATO with no more than four members who are also the trustees of the fund.

Superannuation guarantee charge (SGC) A penalty imposed by the ATO when an employer fails to make a super contribution.

Superannuation guarantee system (SGS) A compulsory superannuation contribution system that requires employers to make a 9 per cent super contribution for all employees earning more than $450 a month.

Super Choice A system introduced under the Howard Government, designed to create more choice and flexibility for superannuation fund members in what super fund their super contributions go to.

Supply A supply is any goods sold or services rendered by an enterprise. The GST act defines it in such broad terms that virtually nothing escapes the GST net. It includes normal business income, such as sales or the provision of services, and the leasing of premises or equipment. It also includes such things as:

- goods being exchanged, as occurs with bartering
- the granting of permission to use something like a property or a car
- the agreement not to do something, such as a restrictive covenant not to sell goods or services in a particular area.

Tax file number (TFN) The unique number issued to taxpayers to identify them by the ATO.

Tax invoice A tax invoice is a document in a prescribed form that must be issued by a supplier within 28 days of a request by a customer. Tax invoices must be retained by a business so that it can claim an input tax credit for the GST paid.

Tax offset Tax concessions that reduce the amount of tax payable by someone. They are not tax deductions, which decrease taxable income: they are reductions in the final tax paid by an individual.

Tax period A tax period is the length of time covered by a BAS for an enterprise. The majority of small businesses have a tax period of three months for PAYG instalments. Where a business has a turnover of more than $20 million a year, however, the PAYG instalments tax period is one month. The tax period for PAYG withholding is quarterly for annual amounts under $25 000 and monthly where the annual amount is between $25 000 and $1 million.

Tax rebate *see* tax offset.

Turnover An accounting term that means the income of a business. When the cash method of accounting is used, annual turnover is the total income collected for a year. Under the accrual method of accounting, annual turnover means the total income invoiced or charged for a year.

Index

Resources

Legislation 328-115(3) on page 35 © Commonwealth of Australia 2008. All legislation herein is reproduced by permission but does not purport to be the official or authorised version. It is subject to Commonwealth of Australia copyright. *The Copyright Act 1968* permits certain reproduction and publication of Commonwealth legislation and judgements. In particular, section 182A of the Act enables a complete copy to be made by or on behalf of a particular person. For reproduction or publication beyond that permitted by the Act, permission should be sought in writing. Requests should be addressed to Commonwealth Copyright Administration, Attorney-General's Department, Robert Garran Offices, National Circuit, Barton ACT 2600, or posted at http://www.ag.gov.au/cca.

Table 7.1: fringe benefits tax rates on cars from 'Fringe benefits tax (FBT) rates and thresholds', ATO, February 2008, copyright Commonwealth of Australia, reproduced with permission.

Table 8.1: GST credit claimable on cars from GST Bulletin 'GSTB2000/2 — How to claim input tax credits for car expenses', ATO, 9/6/2000, copyright Commonwealth of Australia, reproduced by permission.

Table 1: tax rates for individuals (appendix) from 'Individual income tax rates', ATO, July 2007, copyright Commonwealth of Australia, reproduced by permission.

Table 6: minimum superannuation pension rates (appendix) from 'Key superannuation rates and thresholds', ATO, 2007, copyright Commonwealth of Australia, reproduced by permission.

Table 11: statutory car FBT rates (appendix) from 'Claiming a deduction for car expenses using the cents for kilometre method', ATO, June 2007, copyright Commonwealth of Australia, reproduced by permission.

Table 13: GST claimable on car costs under statutory method (appendix) from GST Bulletin 'GSTB2000/2 — How to claim input tax credits for car expenses', ATO, 9/6/2000, copyright Commonwealth of Australia, reproduced by permission.

CCH's excellent tax library, including *The Australian income tax guide*.
The National Tax and Accountants' Association 2008 fringe benefits
    tax seminar notes.
Professor Scott Holmes & Brian Gibson, 'Definition of small business:
    final report', The University of Newcastle, 2001.

Google proved to be a great help in tracking down the various facts and
figures I needed.

The websites for the revenue offices in each state and territory have
a wealth of information on the taxes, duties and charges administered
by them.

The ATO website <www.ato.gov.au> is a great source of help and
has all of the forms needed, along with information sheets that explain
many of the tax issues. If you feel adventurous and want to take a look
at the dark side, the site also has tax-office rulings and goes into the legal
reasons for why the ATO wants to take your money.